ANIMAL ICONS IN WORSHIP
-A nudge at life's purpose-

ANIMAL ICONS IN WORSHIP
-A nudge at life's purpose-

Monica Das

BLACK EAGLE BOOKS
Dublin, USA | Bhubaneswar, India

Black Eagle Books
USA address:
7464 Wisdom Lane
Dublin, OH 43016

India address:
E/312, Trident Galaxy, Kalinga Nagar,
Bhubaneswar-751003, Odisha, India

E-mail: info@blackeaglebooks.org
Website: www.blackeaglebooks.org

First International Edition Published by
Black Eagle Books, 2023

ANIMAL ICONS IN WORSHIP
-A nudge at life's purpose-
by **Monica Das**

Copyright © Monica Das

All rights reserved. No part of this publication may be reproduced, stored in a retrieval system, or transmitted, in any form or by any means, electronic, mechanical, photocopying, recording or otherwise without the prior permission of the publisher.

Cover Art: **Jatin Das**
Interior Design: Ezy's Publication

ISBN- 978-1-64560-400-6 (Paperback)
Library of Congress Control Number: 2023939481

Printed in the United States of America

Foreword

Our lives are intricately linked to the natural world. In India, our cultures and tradition and the heritage they bestow have been shaped over thousands of years by natural habitats and the diversity of species they sustain.

Monica Das' book *Animal Icons* is a welcome reminder of the longstanding relationship that exists between nature and the cultures of the world. In its content, the book celebrates the natural world in an unusually thoughtful way and leads to reimagine, rethink, and rebuild our relationship with nature. Amongst various thoughts of the book – the theme of ahimsa, the tradition and thought of the Panchtantra and that of the oneness of life and the environment - come together and lead a gentle message for the conservation of our natural world.

Monica Das examines the forms of animal worship across world cultures to highlight the manner in which animals have provided a backdrop for our cultural lives for centuries. And by doing so, she highlights an important truth—when we conserve animals, we conserve our cultures and ensure the balance of nature so important for our earth.

The book helps to raise consciousness of the intimate relationship between man and the animal world. Monica Das' effort in generating a sensitivity in this direction is commendable. Reading this book will no doubt be an enriching experience.

Ravi Singh
Secretary General & CEO, WWF-India

ACKNOWLEDGEMENT

I am delighted and honored to have a foreword written for my book on 'Animal Icons' by Mr Ravi Singh who is none other than the CEO of WWF (World Wildlife Fund), Delhi India. I take it as an endorsement to the appeal, I make through this book, concerning animals. His support for this book speaks of his sincerity towards the cause of animal preservation and undoubtedly rings so true of his nature as a genuinely humane person. My sincere gratitude to him. I also wish to thank S Y Quraishi, former Chief Election Commissioner of India, for his unstinting encouragement. He is one who invariably supports all kinds of work that come with a cause and are life affirming. I am also obliged to the Internationally renowned painter artist Jatin Das (Padma Bhushan), for drawing a sketch to grace the cover page of my book. All this is rather reassuring for me. I also thank Indumati Das, a computer engineer who resides in the US for her useful tips while I was writing the blurb. The book was accorded a fine tuning during my stay in California. I thank my son and husband for their continued moral support.

    I would particularly like to mention the name of Geeta Das an educationist who lives and teaches in Bhubaneswar and acted as a springboard for me. I could bounce my ideas with her comfortably. She is not just that but a committed environmentalist. She has zealously helped me edit my work. I am yet to find a person who can be so passionately involved with the work that he or she takes up. I am deeply thankful to her. Last but not the least my thanks to the publisher of the book Mr Satya Pattanaik who resides in the USA. His positive nod and support from day one has given me the right fillip to go ahead with the writing of this book. It is a book with a purpose, the purpose apart from other things is to sensitize the youth regarding planetary crises as well as to impress upon them about the importance of animals for human existence. Hence to have young school children from Odisha, India doing the line drawings of animals for my book definitely works as a bonus for me. I thank them profusely. It is my ardent appeal to readers for giving a dedicated reading to this book and sustaining the cause of saving the planet in their own thoughtful ways.

Monica Das

CONTENTS

PROLOGUE 1

AUTHOR'S NOTE 5
De Profundis

CHAPTER 1 9
Zoolatry is a universal concept: The how and why of it.

CHAPTER 2 16
The Practice of Zoolatry in Greece, Rome, Egypt Arabian Peninsula and China

CHAPTER 3 29
Animals Considered Sacred Universally

CHAPTER 4 38
Animals Commonly Revered and Worshiped

CHAPTER 5 65
Hybrid Animal Icons

CHAPTER 6 77
The Indian Context

CHAPTER 7 90
The Indian Context: Religion and Conservation

CHAPTER 8 107
Animals as Vahanas of Deities

CHAPTER 9 115
Important Temples of Animal Worship in India

CHAPTER 10 124
Preservation of Nature: Promotion of Biodiversity - A Life-Affirming Fact

EPILOGUE 127
Back to Roots

About the Author 133

PROLOGUE

A peep into the records of humans, from prehistoric through the classical and modern periods is filled with examples of animals helping to shape our understanding of ourselves. As is well known approximately 13.5 billion years ago matter, energy, time and space came into being. This refers to the big bang theory. Animals that resemble humans first appeared 2.5 million years ago and it is an acknowledged fact that 2 million years ago a familiar cast of human characters was encountered in East Africa. They were termed 'homosapiens' - a species of the genus homo (man) and sapiens means-wise. We, the homosapiens, claim to be the wisest and best but whether we like it or not we are members of a large particularly noisy family called the great apes. Our closest living relatives are chimpanzees, gorillas, and Orangutans. Of these the closest are chimpanzees. It is rather interesting to note what Uval Noah Harari has written in his book 'Sapiens - A Brief History of Humankind' - 6 million years ago a single female had two daughters one became the ancestor of all chimpanzees and the other is our grandmother. This revelation is rather stimulating and some may think that it is quite humbling.

In the course of our journey through the book in hand, we shall discover that as a matter of fact, animals are at the core of our living. Animals figure in our traditions, our religions and in our culture, the stories we tell each other and our literature. The Panchatantra, the animal characters in the Bible, the Qur'an, stories from the Arabian nights, animal fables of Aesop, and many more, are all testimony to the level of kinship that man had and still has, with animals.

Even coming to think of the Zodiac signs, it is no doubt an example and compelling instance of the extent to which animals have influenced the imagination of man. So much so that even the constellation of stars in heaven and the sky above, are represented and are read into and accepted as the form of animal insignias. Most of the symbols used in the zodiac represent many animals. The ram, the bull, the lion, the scorpion, the crab, the dolphins, the fish and the mountain goat are all part of the zodiac signs.

If on the one hand, the fierce, forceful and energizing power of some animals captivated the imagination of man, giving birth to The Centaur, the Unicorn, the Sphinx, the Dragon, the Garuda, the Narasimha, Ganesha, on the other, the meek, docile and the gentle like the turtle, the parrot, the dolphins, the fish and many more of the likes were bestowed with divine powers as seen in the mythologies. In between the pages of the book, we will encounter myriad facts concerning man and animals.

The obsession of humans with animals can well draw

 its reason from the origin of humans or as we call them Homosapiens. The origin as one would remember has its fascinating connotation as mentioned earlier in the introduction. Moving on, the reader will also come across the practice and the living tradition of the veneration of animals by humans and the various interesting ways in which animals are worshipped. In fact, the book deals with the association of animals and humans that deeply and widely cover all aspects of life.

Furthermore, the practice of Animal worship amongst communities across the globe even to this day reflects the fact that we are the recipients of a primitive culture. At this stage of civilization where we stand today, with the development of science and technology, reasoning and logic, it is interesting and intriguing to gauge the reasons behind our adherence to continuing with the primordial rituals. Perhaps it is time for us to probe into the justifications for our persistence to hold on to such dogmas.

These are doubts, the answers to which probably hold the key to helping us arrive at a pragmatic perspective on the understanding of, the relevance of animal worship and veneration of animal icons and there are good reasons for all this as would be revealed in the course of the book. Besides all these the book also dwells on the fact of 'chimera' said to have existed ages back which is even to this day endorsed in various scholarly works of literature including the one popularly known as 'Nabagunjara' in Odisha.

The book I would say is a book with a cause. The

cause briefly stated is all about the preservation of the fauna, in the context of conservation of the environment and ecosystem. And, above all a subtle undertone of a feeling of kindness and compassion for animals. To neglect this fact would mean in no uncertain terms that man would be negating himself. It goes without saying that all this has a lot to do with a Buddhist saying 'Esho Funi', meaning 'To be one with nature'.

Nabagunjara Patachitra painting by Shri Kalu Charan Barik.
Photo credit: Abhimanyu Barik

Source: https://fundamatics.net/ecological-consciousness-and-the-tale-of-the-nabagunjara-from-folk-odisha/

Nabagunjara is an imaginary mythological creature that has features of nine different animals signifying the importance of each animal with unique traits. (Refer page 88)

AUTHOR'S NOTE

De Profundis

Of late, have been increasingly concerned about the environment and global warming. Matters concerning animal welfare are overwhelmingly preoccupying my mind. At the same time, I have been feeling overly powerless in making changes that would help. Thankfully, there are people in my life who have encouraged me to make incremental changes in the way we live. Perhaps by working together we all can make a massive dent on the issue in hand. One passing thought that came to my mind was to become an activist in this field but the writer in me promptly suggested that I become an academic activist instead. And voila! There I was, writing a book titled 'Animal Icons In Worship -A nudge at life's purpose-

Recounting the pre-covid days, it was the most beautiful world that we lived and slept in. We slept in one and woke up in another; the world had changed overnight. We woke up to find the world today, a world ridden with sickness, anxiety, hopelessness, despair, and despondence. An incredible change that was overwhelmingly deprecating. Is it that our dreams have to die a hundred deaths?

Humanity, as we see it today, has been engulfed in a sweeping manner of devastation. We are reduced to nothing short of zombies. Stuck to a single thought- the thought of keeping our body intact and functioning; the thought of keeping our body and soul together. Such a life calls for complete seclusion. And so, isolation and detachment are the new normal. The old order has changed.

Love got redefined. If you loved your dear and near ones, your friends, you are to physically distance yourself from them. Physical proximity becomes a big NO-NO! Socializing, the traditional ritualistic age-old practice got suspended unceremoniously. Covid had arrived.

Suddenly, Disney got out of magic, Paris no longer appeared romantic, the Taj Mahal lost its sheen, malls no longer attracted us, temples and mosques were empty, hugs and kisses suddenly became weapons of destruction, and not visiting parents and friends have become acts of love. Beauty, money and power lost their worth and failed to get us the oxygen that we needed at that hour. Humor has touched us at the most unexpected time, now we find humans caged in their homes and animals roaming free in urban spaces and human habitats. What an irony of fate!

We have definitely wronged the planet and this time, it is unforgiving. We have plundered the world, cut down forests, polluted air, and water, rivers and seas, all for our insatiable greed for the things that are material, to the utter disrespect of the tenet 'from each unto his capacity and to each unto his need'. There was a time when these seemed unfashionable but man! Look where you are now!

'Love Thyself' has taken over the Biblical tenet of 'love thy neighbour.' Temples and other places of worship have shut down their doors. God now resides in our hearts - the rightful place.

The writing is loud and clear. The punishment is

dire. This is not from a page of any novel; it is real- a world scenario as we saw it only the other day. Parts of it still linger on. The danger still lurks.

Had Pareto's optimality of greatest good of the greatest numbers been observed, it would have arrested this utterly horrifying situation. Humans have failed us or should we say we have failed ourselves? And so today holistic human welfare is hanging by a slender thread. All around a stark scene stares us in the face. Corona's waves seem to be unrelenting. What do we make of this? Is it a Nemesis for humankind? People dying from lack of oxygen sure is a divine vengeance on the human world.

But thankfully, people are showing signs of rising like a phoenix. Corona brought to the fore the long-awaited realization of the universal truth that 'Service to mankind is service to God'.

But the question is not just to do with humans; the whole issue is also about the animal world, the plant world, in fact, the whole ecosystem. One is reminded of the Buddhist concept *'Esho Funi'*- Oneness of Life and the Environment. The onus is on us; the sooner we realize and act, the better for us. The house that we live in, the earth, shelters other creatures also. We cannot live in isolation. If we wish to live, we must let others live. In fact, our sustenance, and our very lives depend on the well-being of all humanity. Now, the one-world concept complemented by the humanistic bent of mind should be the guiding principle. Sustaining life with a philosophical attitude is the call of the day. Growth and development can take a backseat for a while. De- development might sound like an anathema under normal circumstances, however, that is what is needed now. We have to go back to the basics if we are to put things in place and if we are to usher in the 'new normal'. We have witnessed the Zenith and the Nadir of civilization. The graffiti on the wall says, "Go slow, sample the simple, for nothing is more precious than life." Animals beautifully evoke these feelings with ease. Perhaps it is time to turn to nature, to go back to basics, and go back to God again. Saving the planet, saving all that is beautiful may not sound modern or fashionable, but it surely would promise a better quality of life which is the need of the hour.

The animal world opens up wide vistas of this life-affirming truth. So fascinating is the world of animals that it can help us realize once again what it is to be in tandem with the rhythm of nature. As a matter of fact, the world of animals reveals to us the mystical aspect of life and opens the windows of our minds to spirituality, which is life-preserving and in simple terms, magnificent. The whole idea is to make this world a better place to live in.

To quote Rabindranath Tagore the Nobel laureate:

"The highest education is that which does not merely give us information but makes our life in harmony with all existence."

Monica Das

CHAPTER ONE

Zoolatry: A Universal Concept- the How and Why of it

Zoolatry is animal worship. When, why and how 'animal worship' came about is yet to be deciphered. Studies show that animal worship predates all of the commonly practiced organised religions (both mono and polytheism) today. Zoolatry in some form or the other is found to have existed in all civilizations across the world.

From the beginning man has been in a precarious position in the context of his relationship with animals. The irony is that while beasts were his natural enemies, they were also his necessity since they were the main source of food.
While man could conquer his prey he was vanquished by his predator. It is interesting to reflect on the fact as to whether this complex oddity steered man towards animal worship or maybe this has its basis in the concept, 'Fear begets reverence'. However, no one could have understood it better than the savage man who was in constant fear of wild beasts. The savage man lacked both the strength to endure natural disasters and the power to fight against the

beasts in equal measures. The fight for survival was bloody and fierce. Victories against the beasts who were their natural enemies were celebrated and losses were lamented. Lessons were learnt all through the way of how to keep the wild beast at bay. Every event was rejoiced with dance and lighting of the fire, a cacophony of noise and drum beats, thumping and beating of chest and thighs followed by a banquet cooked from the flesh of the vanquished. The vanquished were venerated; even their act in the fight was glorified; a few pieces of memorabilia, mostly bones, teeth, horns, and nails, were retained. Continuous acts of such kind could have been the forerunner to the rites and rituals of animal worship.

Times changed, and life changed, but the practice continued. And so, we still continue with *'zoolatry'* or Animal worship. Rituals pertaining to the glorification of animal deities or animal sacrifice can be found across civilizations in many societies. In instances where particular gods are worshipped by means of a representative animal, it has resulted in the formation of animal cults, which are further classified as per their inward meaning or outward form and are subject to transformation.

The Greek and Roman polemicists spoke of animal worship, albeit in a pejorative manner. However, animals themselves were not worshipped. It was believed that the sacred power of the deity was carried by the animal and was considered a reincarnation of a deity in animal form.

Diodorus, the great classical author, traced the origin of animal worship in mythology. According to this myth, the gods were compelled to conceal themselves from the giants who posed an immense threat to them, in the guise of animals. Consequently, people began adopting those animals their gods disguised themselves to be, as deities and worshipped them. Interestingly, this practice was not terminated and was continued in spite of their gods have returned to their natural state. Johannes Weissenborn[1] proposed a slightly different version. He said that animal worship was prompted by man's natural curiosity. In essence, the uniqueness and the inability to comprehend the traits of an animal in nature would charm or mystify the primitive man observing it. This perplexity or 'wonder', as a result of the primitive man's observations, would gradually develop into 'adoration'. Therefore, Weissenborn concluded, animal worship originated with primitive man worshipping animals with distinctive traits.

This idea resonates in the core values of the indigenous native peoples of Africa, Australia, Asia and the Americas. All of these tribes across continents believe in admiration, respect and love for animals and this belief reflects in most of their day-to-day actions and activities -their way of living.

Animal symbolism in religious iconography and allegory stands out loud and clear in many other religions including Hinduism, Buddhism, Christianity and the religions of the classical Greeks and Romans also.

To cite one instance, the Greeks associated wisdom with the owl, and the goddess of wisdom, Athena, who was believed to have an affiliation with birds and hence, is frequently represented with an owl. A similar association occurs between Jesus Christ and the Lamb in Christian traditions.

---

1 Johannes Weissenborn, "Animal-Worship in Africa", Journal of the Royal African Society,1906, 5(18).

In fact, a widespread and eclectic depiction of animals are found during the medieval times occupying an important place in the creative and imaginative portrayal of artistry. In due course these representations were consigned to less prestigious surfaces throughout the Gothic period, having first appeared in furniture and as a basis for the embellishment of architectural volumes and surfaces during the Romanesque period. With the passage of time gargoyles and 'funerary' creatures related to tombs and epitaphs started to appear. There are animals on the corbels and stalls as well. Last but not least, mascots for saints and those used as their emblems have new importance.

This creates a strong decorative repertoire for the bestiary. Sometimes the choices of animals are even dictated by decorative needs, which also define motivations. From the bison of the Lascaux caves to Larcat's apocalyptic beast at Assy are attestations of the intimate and at times fictitious interactions that humans have with actual or fantasy creatures.

Furthermore, continuing on the human-animal association we have the Chinese zodiac that allocates an animal and its alleged characteristics to each year in a revolving twelve-year cycle. A  fascinating trivia about the Chinese zodiac is that animals are not connected to constellations that are spanned by the ecliptic plane as in the Western zodiac; instead of months, the entire Chinese 12-part cycle is based on years and each year is assigned to an animal. In the Western astrological configuration also, animal representations of stars and constellations can be found.

Animal worship has been widely practiced in various civilizations and has trickled down to us through centuries. As such, animal icons play a central role in most mythologies. The number of animal icons found around the globe speaks about the important place it holds in our lives even today. Does it point out the larger didactic purposes of these myths relating to animals? For instance, in India, animal worship is a lived tradition. In Hinduism, it is believed that zoolatry is a form of intensified or exaggerated expression of the feeling of adoration for three qualities, brute, strength, and utility, found in the animal kingdom. This feeling is further strengthened by the intense hold that the doctrine of metempsychosis has on the Hindu mind.

The sustenance of our very lives depends entirely on the well-being of all humanity. We work in tandem with our environment, and if this ecological balance is disturbed, it could cause irrevocable catastrophe. This rings absolutely true and even more so now in the present times when we are in the grip of the unrelenting corona pandemic, which has claimed innumerable lives.

The world has shrunk; the world is one. The one-world concept is more acknowledged now than it was ever - it is at a premium now. This concept always existed in the Indian subcontinent, especially in the Hindu belief and culture. The ancient saying that supports this concept can be found in the Sanskrit quote, "Vasudhaiva Kutumbakam", which means 'the entire world is our family'. The need of the hour is to apply this one-world concept, with a humanistic approach to things, that can act as a mantra for sustaining life and living. What else could be a better way to practice spiritualism? The questions that arise as a natural corollary here are: where do animals actually belong in the worldview of that culture, in their cosmogony or historical mythology, and how do these etiological beliefs reflect upon the cultural, social and economic positioning of animals?[23] Animal welfare has become a growing concern affecting the acceptability of the use of animals in agricultural systems in many countries around the world. An earlier Judeo-Christian interpretation of the Bible (1982) that dominion over animals meant that any degree of exploitation was acceptable has changed for most people to mean that each person has responsibility for animal welfare. This view was evident in some ancient Greek writings and has parallels in Islamic teaching. A minority view of Christians, which is a widespread view of Jains, Buddhists, and many Hindus, is that animals should not be used by humans as food or for other purposes. The commonest philosophical positions now, concerning how animals should be treated, are a blend of deontological and utilitarian approaches. Most people think that extremes of poor welfare in animals are unacceptable and that those who keep animals should strive for their better upkeep. Hence animal welfare science, which includes the evaluation of welfare, has developed rapidly.

---

2   Steven H. Lonsdale, Attitudes Towards Animals in Ancient Greece, Cambridge University Press, 2009

3   Animal Welfare in Different Human Cultures, Traditions and Religious Faiths, E. Szűcs, R. Geers, T. Jezierski, E. N. Sossidou, and D. M. Broom, journal of Animal Science, 2012

Court of the Lions in The Alhambra of Granada, Spain so named because of the twelve lions that surround the famous fountain in the palace.[4]

Wall Art depicting Thoth: The ibis headed Egyptian god of writing, magic moon and wisdom.[5]

---

4 Credit: Pablo Ramos- https://unsplash.com/photos/UOn-HLmgALxg
5 Credit: https://discover.hubpages.com/education/thoth

CHAPTER TWO

The Practice of Zoolatry in Greece, Rome, Egypt, Arabian Peninsula and China

Animal worship, per se, has gone through several stages of change. Rock carvings and cave paintings of early prehistoric times have graphics of animals in their original forms like tigers, snakes, dragons, crocodiles, lions and a medley of such animals. Gradually with growing consciousness, admiration of the attributes of animals began to give rise to the imagination that further went on to take varied shapes. Thus we have combination creatures in human-beast or human-bird or even beast-bird-human forms.

GANESHA

Totems from the later stages show images of hybrid or fusion animals mostly of half-animal and half-human like the Ganesha (elephant head with a human body), Centaur (human head with the torso of a horse) and many more of the likes.

At the heart of the human-animal relationship is not only the attitude of humans towards animals but more about its reflection in the treatment of animals.

Studies show that religion and philosophy have, to some extent, been inspired by man's basic disposition towards animals around him. And the body of knowledge thus expounded has in turn beguiled generations of people in almost every civilization.

Between the year 2000 BC through the sixteenth century, central America and Mexico were home to the Mayans, considered as one of the oldest civilizations in the world. A lot of fascinating details have been uncovered about the Mayans and the artefacts that are still there are incredibly motivating. Animals held great significance in the Mayan culture because they believed that the animals and plants were extant before humans. Kinichahau, the sun god of Mayans, was represented by a Jaguar. Black howler monkeys, jaguars, rattlesnakes, armadillos, bats, louses, toads, snakes, owls, wild boars, turtles, rabbits, doves, were the animals that the Mayan culture venerated. To the Mayans, animals possessed human or divine qualities with specific roles. The Mayans understood that animals are resources with deep symbolic, mythological, and religious significance.

Human attitudes towards animals have been influenced by the ancient Greek philosophies addressing the formulation of such terms as *ethos* (ἦθος, ἔθος), *ethics* (δέον) and *moral* (ευδαιμονία). *Ethos* is defined as the character, sentiment, or disposition of a community or people, considered as a natural endowment; the spirit which actuates manners and customs; also, the characteristic tone of an institution or social organization. *Ethos* is a Greek word corresponding roughly to "ethics".

The idea that divinity embodies itself in animals,

such as a deity incarnate, and then lives on earth among human beings is disregarded by Abrahamic religions (Morris, 2000, p. 26). In Independent Assemblies of God and Pentecostal churches, animals have very little religious significance (Schoffeleers, 1985; Peltzer, 1987; Qtd. in Morris, 2000, p. 25). Animals have become less and less important and symbolic in cult rituals and religion, especially among African cultures, as Christianity and Islamic religions have spread. (Morris, 2000, p. 24).

The Egyptian pantheon was especially fond of zoomorphism, with many animals sacred to particular deities cats to Bastet, ibises and baboons to Thoth, crocodiles to Sobek and Ra, fish to Set, mongoose, shrew and birds to Horus, dogs and jackals to Anubis, serpents and eels to *Atum*, beetles to *Khepera*, bulls to *Apis*. Animals were often mummified as a result of these beliefs.

Many religions have considered cattle to be sacred, most famously Hinduism from India and Nepal, along with Zoroastrianism, and ancient Greek and Egyptian religion. Cattle and buf-  falo are respected by many pastoral peoples that rely on the animals for sustenance and the killing of an ox is a sacrificial function (Thomas 1911, p. 51).

The Ancient Egyptians worshipped a great number of deities who were either depicted entirely as cattle, or incorporated cattle features in their appearance. *Hesat*, a goddess of milk and motherhood, was depicted as a full cow, as was *Mehet-weret*, a sky goddess, identified as the Celestial Cow whose body made up the sky, and whose four legs marked the four cardinal directions. Bat (goddess), a goddess of music and dance, was depicted as a woman with bovine ears and horns, as was Hathor, a very major goddess who borrowed a lot of her attributes from Bat. The great antiquity of the worship of Bat is evidenced by her appearance on the Narmer Palette, made by the very first of the dynastic pharaohs. When identified with the Celestial Cow *Mehet-weret*, the sky goddess Nut may also take the form of a cow, as in the Book of the Heavenly Cow. When acting in her role as a heavenly goddess, the mother goddess Isis may also be shown with bovine horns, adopting the traditional headdress of Hathor.

The Egyptians worshipped several gods with the head of a ram, including *Khnum, Heryshaf, Banebdjedet*, Ra (sometimes) and *Kherty. Amun*, the god of Thebes, Egypt, was also associated with the ram, and in later periods was sometimes represented as ram-headed. His worshippers held the ram to be sacred, however, it was sacrificed once a year. Its fleece formed the clothing of the idol (Thomas 1911, p. 52).

Silenus, the Satyrs and the Fauns were either capriform or had some part of their bodies shaped like that of a goat. In northern Europe, the wood spirit, *Leszi*, is believed to have a goat's horns, ears and legs (Thomas 1911, p. 51). A deity known as the Goat of Mendes is associated with the pentagram.

In Greece, Italy, and Egypt, the goat was worshipped in both goat form and phallic form (Neave 1988, p. 8). This type of worship has sometimes been said to have originated from the goat's increased sex drive. One male goat was capable of fertilizing 150 females (Neave 1988, p. 8). The Greek god Pan was depicted as having goat characteristics, such as hooves, horns, and a beard. Along with Pan, the goat was closely related to Dionysus during the Roman era (Neave 1988, p. 8). To honour Dionysus, Romans would tear apart a goat and eat it alive.[citation needed] The goat was commonly associated with the dark arts and the devil. This association was amplified in Egypt during the Middle Ages (Neave 1988, p. 8).[citation needed]

Excavations in Central Asia have revealed ancient ritual goat-burial that show the religious significance of the goat predominantly in the area (*Sidky* 1990, p. 286). These findings have been used as evidence for a goat cult in Asia originating either in the Neolithic or Bronze Ages (Sidky 1990, p. 286).

Dogs have a major religious significance among the Hindus in Nepal and some parts of India. The dogs are worshipped as a part of a five-day Tihar festival that falls roughly in November every year. In Hinduism, it is believed that the dog is a messenger of Yama, the god of death, and dogs guard the doors of Heaven. Socially, they are believed to be the protectors of our homes and lives. In order to please the dogs, they are going to meet at Heaven's doors after death, so they would be allowed into Heaven, people mark the 14th day of the lunar cycle in November as Kukur-Tihar, as it is known in the Nepali language, for the dog's day. This is a day when the dog is worshipped by applying tika (the holy vermilion dot), incense sticks and garlanded generally with marigold flower.

Actual dog worship is uncommon. The *Nosarii* of western Asia are said to worship a dog. The *Karang* of *Java* had a cult of the red dog, with each family keeping one in the house. According to one authority, the dogs are images of  wood which are worshipped after the death of a member of the family and burnt after a thousand days. In Nepal, it is said that dogs are worshipped at the festival called *Khicha Puja*. Among the *Harranians* dogs were sacred, but this was rather as brothers of the *mystae* (Thomas 1911, p. 51).

Dogs in Zoroastrianism[6] are accorded a position next to humans. In fact, in one of the sacred texts of the Parsis, it is mentioned that if only one human is present for a religious ritual requiring two persons, a dog may substitute for the second person and for some rituals the presence of a dog is made compulsory as in burial custom when a dog is brought to the place where the dead are laid so the dog might "cast gaze" on the dead. The event is supposed to have a variety of spiritual advantages. Since the dog's keener senses would be able to pick up on traces of life that a human may overlook, it is thought that the original intent was to make sure that the individual was indeed dead.

The Incas believed that dogs possess supernatural powers. Dogs have the ability to see spirits. Peruvians respect dogs for their mystical powers. Dogs were highly respected and were not only bred and domesticated but adorned with ornaments.

Horse worship has been practised by a number of Indo-European and Turkic peoples. In the nomadic tradition, the horse is one of the mythological animals, embodying the connection with the other world, with the supernatural. The horse, especially white, has always been associated with the sun, with daytime clarity, with fire, air, sky, water, and solar heroes, as an expression of good human aspirations in daily work and struggle against difficulties. The white sun horse is an attribute of divine forces that are constantly fighting against evil, an opposition to death.

---

6   Zoroastrian Attitudes toward Animals Richard Foltz/Society and Animals 18 (2010) 367-378 brill.nl/soan

Additionally, it is said that the water god Poseidon was originally imagined as a horse. The Romans considered both horses and mules to be sacred. A divinity with a horse's head named Hayagriva is revered in both Buddhism and Hinduism. The  Gonds tribe in India likewise reveres a horse that is carved out of stone. In Europe, horses are admired and coveted by the people even today. In Balkan culture, in order to get the power and virility of the animal, a bachelor is wrapped around a horse In Ancient Egypt, there were several feline-shaped deities. The earliest attested of these was the goddess Mafdet. During the First Dynasty of 2920–2770 BC, Mafdet was regarded as the protector of the Pharaoh's chambers against snakes, scorpions and other evil. She was often depicted with the head of a cheetah, leopard or lynx (Hornblower, 1943). In later periods, other feline deities were more dominant. There were several lion-headed deities, that included goddesses such as Sekhmet, Tefnut, Bastet (early form), Pakhet, Mehit and Menhit, and gods such as Maahes.

Of great importance in Chinese myth and culture, the Tiger is one of the twelve Chinese zodiac animals. Some cultures that celebrated tiger worship are still represented contemporarily. In the suburbs of Kunming, China, there is a tourist attraction where the tiger worship of the Yi people is displayed for visitors. This attraction called the Solar Calendar Square is complete with a growling tiger statue, measuring to be five meters high (Harrell & Yongxiang 2003, p. 380). In Chuxiong of China, a similar attraction exists. A tiger totem is presented for tourists; the totem portrays the Yi belief of the tiger setting the entire world in motion. A tiger dance of the Shuangbai County is also performed at such places explaining the history of the Yi and their worship of tigers (Harrell & Yongxiang 2003, p. 380).

The tiger is also associated with the Hindu deities Shiva and Durga. In Kirtipur, Nepal the tiger festival is known as *Bagh Bhairav Jatra* where devotees dance disguised as tigers. The *Warli* tribe of Maharashtra, India worship *Waghia* the lord of tigers in the form of a shapeless stone (Thomas 1911, p. 52). In Vietnamese folk religion and *Dongbei* folk religion, tiger-gods are also found.

Together with the eagle and the hawk, the crow plays a great part in the mythology of southeastern Australia (Thomas 1911, p. 51). Ravens also play a part in some European mythologies, such as in the Celtic and Germanic Religions, where they were connected to Bran and the Morrigan in the former and Wooden in the latter.

In Ancient Egypt, the ibis was considered sacred as it was viewed as a manifestation of Thoth, a god of the moon and wisdom. In art, Thoth was usually depicted as a man with the head of an ibis, or more rarely as a baboon. Sacred ibises were kept and fed in temples in his honour, and mummified ibises were given to him as votive offerings. It is thought that the association of the ibis with Thoth may have originated from the curved shape of the bird's beak, which resembles a crescent moon.

It is interesting to note that along with animals and birds, insects, reptiles and amphibians also occupied a place of reverence in some of the ancient civilizations. Going back to the religion of ancient Egypt again, Sobet, the crocodile god had a significant place in the Egyptian pantheon. Sobet is represented as having the head of a crocodile and the body of a human. In the Geeko-Roman mythology also references to Sobet can be traced. Crocodile totems are found to be commonly used among the aboriginal people of Australia[7]. In Hindu mythology, the crocodile or 'makara' as it is called is depicted as part crocodile and part fish and holds a divine place as the 'Vahana' of Varuna. In Hindu astrology, the Zodiac sign Capricorn is represented by Makara. Instances of Makara in sculpture can be found in Buddhism and Jainism prevalent in Tibet, Sri Lanka, and the South and Southeast Asian countries.

The beetle, the locust, the grasshopper, the scorpion, the butterfly, the flies, the bees and a few more from the insect world have each found a seat of honour in the Bible, the Quran, the Old Testament of the Jews, the ancient Egyptians, Chinese folklores, Japanese culture, the African tribes, the Hindus and many more religions, mythologies of old and the present. Among all these insects, the bee and honey hold an unparalleled position of respect. From the most primitive to the present, the virtue of the bee and the attributes of honey have been extolled in various mythological texts and holy scriptures.

---

7   https://www.earth.com/news/cultures-crocodiles-worshipped/

The Aztec civilization had their empire in the 14th century in a place that is now called Central Mexico. The animals formed a significant part of their world view. Almost all animals that were worshipped by the ancient Aztecs are under some kind of threat in Mexico, according to biologist, 'Carlosgalindo', director of science communication. National Commission for the Knowledge and Use of Biodiversity, Conabio. Galindo adds in his speech on the occasion of Animal Day- "The main problem is that they are forgotten in our minds". One example of their animal god is the deity Quetzalcoati. It is somewhat of a hybrid form- a feathered snake or a snakebird. This is to emphasize the qualities of both the animals.

The Jaguar, the quetzal, hummingbirds and the golden eagle are some of the animals which long before being endangered left their mark on Mexican civilization. They formed part of their customs and were a vital piece in their world view.

Our study so far leads us to believe that man had a thorough knowledge of harnessing animal resources to his advantage way back even in prehistoric times. Why then did man go against the animal kingdom by introducing commercial farming, animal husbandry, deforestation, reckless industrialization, pollution, and so forth? Why did they venerate such animals at the same time? The answer is pretty clear. They were certainly aware of the utility of cows, horses, camels, and elephants, the loyalty of dogs, birds and bees and the virtues of many more animals. Could it be pure greed or a complete lack of understanding of the terrible, far-reaching effects on oneself? These types of questions crop up in our sensitive minds ever so often. In course of time, all this proved detrimental to  humans and the environment at large. In view of these, an in-depth reflection is called for.

The horse pillar in Sri Ranganathaswamy temple, Srirangam, India.[8]

---

8 Credit: Gokul R

The Dragon a popular and highly revered animal icon of South Asia. WiangKumKam Stone Sculpture, Thailand [9]

The Gajasimha structure on both sides of the entrance to Konark Temple, Odisha, India. A lion atop an elephant with a human crushed underneath is symbolic of man being crushed under the combined load of power (lion) and wealth (elephant).[10]

---

9   https://unsplash.com/photos/YT7MkjJ_kTI
10   Credit: Anirudh Pranesh- https://unsplash.com/photos/7Qr-BjYLZf8

Stonework of humans and animals in Angkor Wat, Krong Siem Reap, Cambodia[11]

Watercolour painting of the Popol Vuh, the Quiché Mayan book of creation[12]

---

11   Credit: Ruby Ku- https://unsplash.com/photos/0my_OVsie5c
12   Creation by Diego Rivera. Watercolour painted in San Francisco, California, during the summer of 1931, originally commissioned to illustrate a never-published English translation of the Popol Vuh by John Weatherwax. Courtesy the Library of Congress

CHAPTER THREE

Animals Considered Sacred Universally

Not every animal can be found everywhere on the planet, and not every animal was revered by ancient people. However, there are a few creatures that are common to many regions, such as the cow, goat, snake, bees, and fish, that have been worshipped as gods and goddesses throughout history. Natural selection and elimination, adaptation, and migration of humans and animals expanded the list of venerated animals in due course.

Fables and myths woven around animals give an idea of the intensity of the relationship between animals and humans. As for India, fables found in the Panchatantra, myths around the Holy cow, and the Nandi bull are examples that denote the intensity between animals and humans. Noah's ark from the Bible (western literature) is an instance that instils the importance and the need to preserve animals. Running on similar grounds is a fable from Hindu mythology. So the story goes thus:

Manu saw a small fish crying for help from the waters of the river, one day, as he was sitting and praying by it near his home.

"I am a small and vulnerable fish who is at the mercy of larger fish and other monsters that would hunt me down. Please help me!". Manu felt bad for the small fish. He took it carefully in his hands, lowered it gently into a puddle not far from his hermitage, and made a promise to guard it against all dangers.

The fish had all of its requirements met by Manu, and it soon started to grow. Manu transferred it to a pond and then to the river and finally to the ocean at every stage when the fish outgrew its home. When Manu dropped the fish in the ocean, the fish grew into a gigantic size and said,

"The moment has come, Manu, for me to tell you everything. I'm not just any fish, of course; I'm your Lord Vishnu. All living creatures will perish in a terrifying deluge that will purge the world of all its iniquity. Return to your hermitage and construct a powerful ark. Take the seven sages and their families, the male and female of every animal, and the seeds of all plants into the ship. Please remember to invite Vasuki, the snake God, as well"

Manu constructed the ship keeping in mind to load it with everything the fish had instructed him to do including the sages with their families and Vasuki the snake God. When the deluge came, the fish came to rescue the ship. Vasuki coiled around the horn of the fish fastening itself with the ship. The fish steered the ship and lodged it atop Mount Himavat until the water receded and it was safe. Manu is attributed to have been the first king who preserved life from extinction in a devastating flood. Another interesting narrative is that of the bull-man from the Sumerian civilization.

In Sumeria, Kusarikku had a human head and torso, with bovine ears and horns and hindquarters and is known as the Bull Man. He is a doorkeeper to protect the inhabitants from malevolent intruders and evil spirits. He is associated with the God of Justice. What an apt way to say that animals are our protectors!

In Greek tradition, a Sphinx is a mythical creature with the head of a human and the body of a lion and sometimes the wings of a bird. Those who cannot answer its riddle are killed and eaten. Unlike the Greek sphinx, the Egyptian sphinx is male, benevolent, and with ferocious strength. Both are guardians flanking the entrances to temples and tombs.

Each of these Egyptian Gods has the head of a lion. Maahes is an ancient Egyptian lion-headed god of war, protection, weather, knives, lice, and devouring captives. Pakhet is a lioness-headed deity associated with flash floods. Sekhmet is a warrior goddess as well as the goddess of healing. It was said that her breath formed the desert. She was seen as the protector of the pharaohs. Tefnut is the goddess of moisture, moist air, dew, and rain. Married to her brother Shu, she is the mother of Nut, the sky and Geb, the earth. Temples of Sobet, the crocodile-headed god and many mummies of crocodiles being excavated prove the prevalence of the reptile being worshipped.

In the Arabian Peninsula, before the rise of Islamism, the fact that many tribes bear the names of animals may only imply the practice of totemism and animal cult. People of the Bedouin tribe associated animals with the qualities and attributes of human beings. Totems of pre-Islam nomadic tribes of Arabia reflect the practice of Animism, a system in which non-human entities (animals, plants, and inanimate objects or phenomena) possess a spiritual essence. As such animals were revered; but then they were slaughtered too. In the arid desert regions where vegetation is scanty man is left with no option other than killing animals for food.

Amongst the followers of Islamism kindness and compassion for animals are ordained in their holy texts. Slaughter of animals other than for food is banned. The Quran contains many verses on animals and there are particularly six chapters that are named after animals. An interesting fact mentioned in the Qur'an is that the animals have a distinct community of their own and each animal has a father, mother, sister, brother, uncles, aunts and neighbours as we have. Also that all beasts are Muslims and humans are to treat them with respect befitting a fellow Muslim.

A deep-rooted human-animal kinship is what the Native American belief is all about. A remarkable characteristic of American Native Indian culture is their view on the origin of the cosmos. According to them, the agents of creation are forces of nature (such as wind/breath) or animal-like beings (coyote, raven, great white hare, and a few other animals possessing spiritual powers or a holy being depicted as "wakan" or the great spirit. For them, the four-legged and the winged, the earth with mountains, springs and rivers, and the forests with trees, flowers and fruits are like our relatives, our mother, grandmother and great-grandmother. Creation is beautiful and so everything in it has to be respected, admired and loved.

Hinduism specifically considers the *zebu* (Bos indicus) to be sacred. Respect for the lives of animals including cattle, diet in Hinduism and vegetarianism in India is based on Hindu ethics. Hindu ethics is driven by the core concept of Ahimsa, i.e. non-violence towards all beings, as mentioned in the *Chandogya Upanishad* (~ 800 BCE). By the mid-1st millennium BCE, all three major religions – Buddhism, Hinduism, and Jainism -- were championing non-violence as an ethical value, and something that impacted one's rebirth. According to *Harris*, by about 200 CE, food and feasting on animal slaughter were widely considered a form of violence against life forms and became a religious and social taboo. India, which has a 79.80% Hindu population as of (the 2011 census), had the lowest rate of meat consumption in the world according to the 2007 UN FAO statistics, and India has more vegetarians than the rest of the world put together.

It is customary to regard the Vedas as the inspirational source of the entire Indian way of life and thought. During the prehistoric days of sparse population and difficult inter-communication, the great diversity of the cultural life of people in India can easily be imagined. And that explains the diverse view about gods prevalent among the *rishis* (sages). Getting to think from such a perspective, one is led to believe that every form of Fetishism and Totemism, of stone worship, tree worship, and animal worship, as well as every variety of polytheistic and pantheistic superstition, burgeoned spontaneously and flourished vigorously on the Indian soil.

It is held by some that for a Hindu, zoolatry is the expression of an exaggerated or intensified feeling of admiration for the three qualities; utility, brute strength, and instinct that manifest in animal nature. It must be remembered, too, that for a Hindu, all organic life is sacred. This feeling is strengthened by the intense hold that the doctrine of metempsychosis has on the Hindu mind. The worship of iconic animals is part of the lived tradition in India. The heritage of Hinduism has been described by some as the heritage of eternal truths intuited in the inspired depths of a mystic moment and transmitted with timeless relevance. Traditional practices and animal worship are integral parts of the daily life of an average Indian.

Guardian lions stand on either side of the temple entrances in Asia.

Statue of Lion in Angkor Wat, Krong Siem Reap, Cambodia.[13]

---

13   Credit: Norbert Braun- https://unsplash.com/photos/TYc-CB_WhUrI

Lion statue at The Grand Palace, Wat Phra Kaew, Temple of the Emerald Buddha in Bangkok, Thailand.[14]

The Tiger cave is one of the structures in the complex of temples and shrines of Mahabalipuram, Tamil Nadu, India. Entrance to the cave is circled with tiger head carvings.[15]

---

14   Credit: Rob King- https://unsplash.com/photos/ur89YgSlEGE
15   Credit: https://en.m.wikipedia.org/wiki/Tiger_Cave_(India)

Hieroglyphs and carvings depicting Egyptian gods with animal heads and human body in Temple of Luxor, Egypt.[16]

Statues of birds and animals adorn the roof of Jokhang Temple House in Lhasa.[17]

---

16   Credit: AXP Photography- https://unsplash.com/photos/58jlQxHMzqQ
17   Credit: Raimond Klavins- https://unsplash.com/photos/nqgdeJX1EXY

Sphinx, a mythical creature with the head of a human, and the body of a lion. Great Sphinx & pyramids of Giza, Egypt.[18]

Serpent worship is an integral part of Hindu religion and culture. The Mannarasala Temple in Kerala, India.[19]

---

18   Credit: Nataliia Blazhko- https://unsplash.com/photos/s-MrMrRSE8E
19   Credit: AussieActive- https://unsplash.com/photos/oTRD-P4nU8Q

CHAPTER FOUR

Animals Commonly Revered and Worshipped

As modern man grapples with issues like the dwindling population of the fauna around us, the revival of age-old practices of our ancestors honouring animals, some still living and many lost can hold an answer towards sustainability. Though critics pin on the practices of animal sacrifices by our ancestors, advocates cite several customs that were particularly meant for preservation and conservation. What is important is to hold on to such traditions which are relevant now.

As discussed earlier on in this book, not all animals of the entire animal kingdom had the privilege of being sanctified. Only a few could manage to occupy the seats of reverence and a place amongst the gods.

Snakes

In Egyptian mythology, the cobra-headed *Meretseger*, meaning "she who loves silence", exerted [20]great authority and was considered to be both a dangerous and merciful goddess. She spat venom at anyone who tried to *vandalise* or rob the royal tombs. Gorgons were women with snakes

---

20 https://www.firstpost.com/living/animals-in-divinity-human-beings-have-been-worshipping-animals-in-religion-for-a-very-long-time-4230877.html

instead of hair. In Greek mythology, their powerful gaze could turn one to stone.

The worship of the serpent is found in many parts of the Old World, and in the Americas (Thomas 1911, p. 52).

In India, snake worship refers to the high status of snakes in Hindu mythology. Over a large part of India, there are carved representations of cobras (*nagas*) or stones as substitutes. To these humans, food and flowers are offered and lights are burned before the shrines. Among the *Dravidians* a cobra which is accidentally killed is burned like a human being; no one would kill one intentionally. The serpent god's image is carried in an annual procession by a celibate priestess (Thomas 1911, p. 52). At one time there were many prevalent different renditions of the serpent cult located in India. In Northern India, a masculine version of the serpent named *Nagaraja* and known as the "king of the serpents" was worshipped. Instead of the "king of the serpents," actual live snakes were worshipped in South India (*Bhattacharyya* 1965, p. 1). The *Manasa cult* in Bengal, India, however, was dedicated to the anthropomorphic serpent goddess, *Manasa* (Bhattacharyya 1965, p. 1).

The Ancient Egyptians believed that serpents had both positive and negative representations. On the one hand, the Egyptians worshipped a number of beneficent snake deities, including *Wadjet*, *Renenutet*, *Meretseger*, *Nehebkau* and *Mehen*. The uraeus was a fierce divine cobra that protected Egyptian kings and major deities. On the other hand, the serpent Apophis was a malevolent demon, who endeavoured to destroy the chief deity Ra. The Sumerians had a serpent god *Ningizzida*.

For most of us the word 'snakes' conjures up images of lurking danger, venom and of destruction. The Hebrews worshipped serpents. Mexicans also worship serpents and have exalted the snake to a deity. So, snakes have evoked feelings of both awe and veneration in the minds of the people of the world. H. Zimmer holds that among the motifs from early Mesopotamian art is the pattern of the entwined serpent pair. This pattern is also found on votive stone slabs called *Nagakols* which are used by women desiring offspring. In Mesopotamia, this pattern appears on the sacrificial goblet of King *Gudea* of Lagash. The Delphi sanctuary of the God Apollo was the most important seat of divination in ancient Greece. Here a mound of stone not only represented the centre of the world but also marked the grave of a murdered python. Coming back to a more familiar terrain: the *Sumangli* in south India every day after her morning bath, draws, with powdered rice, the *Nagakolam* (the snake pattern) at the main entrance to her house. Have we ever wondered why? Why does medical science, even up to the present era use, as its emblem the symbol of entwined serpents?

Why does the hood of a snake tower over the *Shivlinga*? Why did Cleopatra, the paragon of beauty, choose such an unusual way to breathe her last using a serpent to bite her breast? Why does the snake occupy such a prominent position in the Hindu religion? On the occasion of *Bhoomi Pujan*, when the foundation of a building is laid, a pair of silver snakes is consecrated to the earth that has been dug up and an ovation is offered to *Sheshnag* the king cobra, who it is believed, carries the weight of the earth on his body This is probably done to appease the holy subterranean reptile lest it feels offended or disturbed since the balance of its domain has been tampered with. This practice is very commonly followed in most of the northern parts of India and even in the metropolis of Delhi. In Puri, Odisha, there is a place called *Charisri*, where small and big cobras live in perfect harmony with humans so much so that they even share the same bed! And in *Charisri*, it is said that not one single man or woman has been bitten by a snake to date. It is widely believed in *Charisri*, that it is the *Jodalingam* (dual phallic symbol of Lord Shiva), because  of whose benevolence, such a phenomenon exists. Hymns of the Rigveda may be silent on serpent worship, but the Yajurveda and especially the Atharvaveda, definitely mention it. The same is true of later Vedic literature. As far as the Indus Valley and Harappan cultures go, despite the great importance accorded to animal worship, there is surprisingly enough, no seal of Harappan culture that encapsulates the figure of a serpent has been found. Crocodiles are there but the serpent is missing, though both belong to the reptile family. The great epic Mahabharata is very rich in myths relating to *nagas* (snakes). It narrates how *Kadru*, wife of the sage *Kasyapa*, became the mother of one thousand *nagas*, who in turn became progenitors of the whole serpent race. *Seshnaga* was *Kadru's* oldest child. Mansa is as popular as any other defy and *Nagpanchami*, a festival held on the fifth day of the month of *Shrawan*, is celebrated in Bengal with much pomp and gaiety. In the State of Assam in India, the *Badai* earn their livelihood through snakes.

Serpents have held men in their spell throughout the world. Many nations still practice snake worship. Hindus have voluminous serpent lore. The king of the serpent gods is *Anantha*, the thousand-headed hydra, who forms a couch for Vishnu. Shiva's personal embellishments include a serpent as a sacred thread. Another serpent in his girdle and his hair tied in a knot and put in place by means of a serpent. He has serpents for bangles and serpents for anklets. A figure of Ganesha, which has an inscription in Brahmi characters and belongs to the 7th century AD and is now kept as an object of a cult at *Pir Ratan Nauh Dargah*, Kabul, shows Ganesha bearing a snake as the Yagnopavita (the sacred thread) hanging across his chest. Buddhism also has its association with serpents. *Patala*, the netherworld, is the habitat of the great serpents of Hindu lore. Serpent tales speak of *Bhogavati*, the capital of the serpent kingdom which is built mainly of precious stones and is the richest city in the 14 worlds. Even the New Testament extols the wisdom of the serpent. In certain parts of India, child deaths are attributed to the wrath of serpents and women desiring offspring of their own obsecrate snakes with elaborate rituals. *Bana Bhattas Kadambari* has a strong reference to rituals amongst which her bath in *naga* ponds figures prominently. All this points to the belief in the fecundating ability of the serpent and its phallic symbolism. The snake cult in India is unfathomable. It is so vast that one can literally go round and round in circles! The snake in turn cannot help but be charmed by the music of man. Talking of music serpent and man, the *Raga Mala*, a series of Indian miniature paintings comes to mind. Here *Ragini Asavari* is described as a goddess frequenting the *Malaya* Mountain and luring the serpents entwined around sandalwood trees while *Ragini Ahiri* is described as a damsel engaged in feeding milk to serpents and so as we sing the song of the serpent, the close association of man and snake lives on.

Another animal that has a universal presence is the fish.

Fish

Going by Hindu mythology, the Fish is associated with the beginning of creation. The fish is the mount of Varuna and Ganga. **Matsya**, (Sanskrit: "Fish"), one of the 10 avatars (incarnations) of the Hindu god Vishnu. In this appearance, Vishnu saved the world from a great flood. Manu, the first man, caught a little fish that grew to a giant size. When the flood approached, Manu saved himself by tying his boat to the horn on the fish's head. It is interesting to note that the fish incarnation is also associated with a similar mythical story from Sumerian and later Hebrew folklore. According to some scholars, the fish sign in the Indus script signifies God. Fish is used on important occasions like marriages in the coastal districts of Bengal and Odisha, which are predominantly fish-consuming communities. They have a large fish sent to the prospective bride, a day before the wedding and along with this is also sent a fish-shaped sweetmeat called *sandesh*. In Uttar Pradesh, in a particular month of the year, a religious ceremony is organized where an artificial fish pond is created in the courtyard of the house. Fish, therefore, is more than just passing symbols in Indian folklore. They are part of our living heritage.

In the story of the great flood, Manu[21] combines the characteristics of the Hebrew Bible figures of Noah, who preserved life from extinction in a great flood, and Adam, the first man. The *Shatapatha Brahmana* recounts how he was warned by a fish, to whom he had done kindness, that a flood would destroy the whole of humanity. He, therefore, built a boat, as per the advice of the fish. When the flood came, he tied this boat to the fish's horn and was safely steered to a resting place on a mountaintop. When the flood receded, Manu, the sole human survivor, performed a sacrifice, pouring oblations of butter and sour milk into the waters. After a year there was born from the waters a woman who announced herself as "the daughter of Manu." These two then became the ancestors of a new human race to replenish the earth. In the *Mahabharata* ("Great Epic of the Bharata Dynasty"), the fish is identified with the god Brahma, while in the *Puranas* ("Ancient Lore") it is Matsya, an incarnation of Lord Vishnu.

In Japan, there was a deity called Ebisu-gami who, according to *Sakurada Katsunori*, was widely revered by fishing communities and industries (Qtd. in Naumann, 1974, p. 1). Ebisu, in later traditions, normally appeared in the form of a fisherman holding a fishing pole and carrying a red Tai (a perch), but would sometimes take the form of a whale, shark, human corpse, or rock (Naumann, 1974, p. 1). The general image of Ebisu, however, appears to be the whale or the shark, according to Sakurada (Qtd. in Naumann, 1974, p. 2).

Cows

Several scholars explain the veneration for cows among Hindus (in economic terms, including the impor-

---

21 From Encyclopaedia Britannica on Manu

tance of dairy in the diet, the use of cow dung as fuel and fertilizer, and the importance that cattle have historically played in agriculture). Ancient texts such as Rig Veda, Puranas highlight the importance of cattle. The scope, extent and status of cows throughout ancient India is a subject of debate. According to D. N. Jha, cattle, including cows, were neither inviolable nor as revered in ancient times as they were later. A *Gryhasutra* recommends that beef be eaten by the mourners after a funeral ceremony as a ritual rite of passage. In contrast, according to Marvin Harris, the Vedic literature is  contradictory, with some suggesting ritual slaughter and meat consumption, while others suggesting a taboo on meat eating.

Many ancient and medieval Hindu texts debate the rationale for a voluntary stop to cow slaughter and the pursuit of vegetarianism as a part of a general abstention from violence against others and the killing of all animals.

The interdiction of the meat of the bounteous cow as the food was regarded as the first step to total vegetarianism. Dairy cows are called *aghnya* "that which may not be slaughtered" in Rigveda. *Yaska*, the early commentator of the Rigveda, gives nine names for cows, the first being *"aghnya"*. According to Harris, the literature relating to cow veneration became common in the 1st millennium CE, and by about 1000 CE vegetarianism, along with a taboo against beef, became a well-accepted mainstream Hindu tradition. This practice was inspired by the beliefs in Hinduism that a soul is present in all living beings, life in all its forms is interconnected, and non-violence towards all creatures is the highest ethical value. Vegetarianism is a part of the Hindu culture. Lord Krishna and his Yadav kinsmen are associated with the tending of cows, adding to their endearment.

In Puranas, which are part of the Hindu texts, the earth-goddess Prithvi was in the form of a cow, successively milked of beneficent substances for the specific benefit of humans. A story has it that starting with the first sovereign Prithu was the one that milked the cow to generate crops for humans in order to end a famine. *Kamadhenu*, the miraculous "cow of plenty" and the "mother of cows" in certain versions of the Hindu mythology, is believed to represent the generic sacred cow, regarded as the source of all prosperity. In the 19th century, a form of *Kamadhenu* was  depicted in poster art that depicted all major gods and goddesses in it. *Govatsa Dwadashi* which marks the first day of Diwali celebrations is the main festival connected to the veneration and worship of cow as the chief source of livelihood and religious sanctity in India, wherein the symbolism of motherhood is most apparent with the sacred cow *Kamadhenu* and her daughter Nandini.

The reverence for the cow played a role in the Indian Rebellion of 1857 against the British East India Company. Hindu and Muslim sepoys in the army of the East India Company came to believe that their paper cartridges, which held a measured amount of gunpowder, were greased with cow and pig fat. The consumption of swine is forbidden in Islam and Judaism. Because loading the gun required biting off the end of the paper cartridge, they concluded that the British were forcing them to break the edicts of their religion.

A historical survey of major communal riots in India between 1717 and 1977 revealed that 22 out of 167 incidents of rioting between Hindus and Muslims were attributable directly to cow slaughter.

Cow protection was a symbol of animal rights and of non-violence against all life forms for Gandhi. He venerated cows and suggested ending cow slaughter to be the first step to stopping violence against all animals. He said: "I worship it and I shall defend its worship against the whole world" and stated that "The central fact of Hinduism is cow protection."

Jainism is against violence to all living beings, including cattle. According to the *Jaina sutras*, humans must avoid all killing and slaughter because all living beings are fond of life, they suffer, feel pain, like to live, and long to live. All beings should help each other life and prosper, according to Jainism, not kill and slaughter each other.

In the Jain religious tradition, neither monks nor laypersons should cause others or allow others to work in a slaughterhouse. Jains believe that vegetarian sources can provide adequate nutrition, without creating suffering for animals such as cattle. According to some Jain scholars, slaughtering cattle increases the ecological burden from human food demands since the production of meat entails intensified grain demands, and reducing cattle slaughter by 50 per cent would free up enough land and ecological resources to solve all malnutrition and hunger worldwide.

The Jain community leaders states Christopher Chapple, "have actively campaigned to stop all forms of animal slaughter including cattle".

The texts of Buddhism state ahimsa to be one of five ethical precepts, which requires a practising Buddhist to "refrain from killing living beings". Slaughtering cows has been taboo. Cattle are seen in some Buddhist sects as a form of reborn human beings in the endless rebirth cycles in samsara, protecting animal life and being kind to cattle and other animals is good karma. Not only do some, but mainly Mahayana, Buddhist texts also state that killing or eating meat is wrong, it urges Buddhist laypersons to not operate slaughterhouses, nor trade in meat. Indian Buddhist texts encourage a plant-based diet.

According to *Saddhatissa*, in the *Brahmanadhammika Sutta*, the Buddha "describes the ideal mode of life of *Brahmins* in the Golden Age" before him as follows: Like mother (they thought), father, brother or any other kind of kin, cows are our kin most excellent from whom come many remedies. Buddha[22]

While there are several animals that are worshipped in India, the supreme position is held by the cow[23]. The humped zebu, a breed of cow, is central to the religion of Hinduism[24]. Mythological legends have supported the sanctity of the zebu throughout India[25]. Such myths have included the creation of a divine cow mother and cow heaven by the God, Brahma and Prithu, the sovereign of the universe, who created the earth's vegetation, edible fruits and vegetables, disguised as a cow[26].

---

22 Brahmanadhammika Sutta 13.24, Sutta Nipāta
23 Margul, 1968, p. 63
24 Margul, 1968, p. 63
25 Margul, 1968, p. 64
26 Margul, 1968, p. 64

From The significance of cows in Indian society between sacredness and economy. The cow is the most sacred of all the animals of Hinduism. It is known as *Kamadhenu*, or the divine cow, and the  giver of all desires. According to legend, she emerged from the ocean of milk at the time of *samudramanthan* or the great churning of the ocean by the gods and demons. She was presented to the seven sages, and in the course of time came into the custody of sage Vasishta, the teacher of Ram (hero of the epic *Ramayana*). Her legs symbolize four Vedas; her nipples four *Purushartha* (or objectives, i.e., *dharma* or righteousness, *artha* or material wealth, *kama* or desire and moksha or salvation); her horns symbolize the gods, her face the sun and moon, and her shoulders *agni* or the god of fire. She has also been described in four other forms: *Nanda, Sunanda, Surabhi, Susheela* and *Sumana* (*Ganapathi* 2005). Legends also state that Brahma gave life to priests and cows at the same time so that the priests could recite religious scriptures while cows could offer *ghee* (clarified butter) as offerings in rituals. Anyone who kills cows or allows others to kill them is deemed to rot in hell for as many years as there are hairs upon his body. Likewise, the bull is depicted as a vehicle of Lord Shiva: a symbol of respect for the male cattle. The *Nandi* (bull) located at the Shiva temples at *Thanjavur, Rameshwaram* and *Mahabalipuram* are the most venerated bovine shrines in Tamil Nadu State of southern India. Similarly, large numbers of pilgrims also visit the 16th-century bull temple at Bangalore (Karnataka State) and 11th century Nandi temple at *Kajuraho* (Madhya

Pradesh State). The Vishwanath temple of Jhansi built in 1002 AD also harbours a large bull (Ganapathi 2005). The cow was revered as a mother goddess in Mediterranean civilizations. The cow became celebrated in India, first during the Vedic period (1500–900 BCE) as a symbol of wealth. Bulls were sacrificed to the gods, and people ate their meat. Nonetheless, the slaughter of milk-producing cows was prohibited. The Rig Veda refers to the cow as devi or goddess. Although meat-eating was permitted in the Vedic period, the scriptures encourage vegetarianism. An example is the Laws of Manu, which states that there is no sin in eating meat, but abstention brings great rewards[27]. In the *Mahabharata, Bhishma* (grandfather of the leaders of warring factions) observes that the cow acts as a surrogate mother by providing milk to human beings for a lifetime, so she is truly the mother of the world. The *Puranas* state that nothing is more religious than the gift of cows. In the epic Ramayana, Rama was given a dowry of many cows when he married Sita[28].

The sanctity of cows may have been based on economic reasons. During the Vedic period, cattle played a significant source of wealth for the predominant pastoral communities, which is similar to the Masai tribe in East Africa today. The five key "products" of the cow include milk, curds, ghee butter, urine, and dung; they are used in daily lives[29]. Cows provide milk that helps to sustain the lives of adults and children. The milk by-products such as yoghurt, buttermilk, butter, and ghee are an integral part of people's daily diet in India. Cow dung is widely used for fuel in rural areas; people also use the dung to clean and plaster house floors and walls; cow dung has been

27   Buhler 1964
28   *Dutt* 2009
29   *Govindasamy Agoramoorthy*, Minna J. Hsu

scientifically proven to have antiseptic value. Hindus do not share the Western repulsion towards cow excrement, but instead, consider it a natural beneficial product. Being tame, cattle are an excellent beast of burden; they pull carts and plough the field to plant crops. Even after death, their skin is useful to a human.

The cow remains a revered and protected animal in Hinduism today and people of the Hindu faith refrain from eating beef. Most rural families across India have at least one dairy cow. Despite their sacred status, cows do not appear to be much appreciated in the day-to-day lives of people in India. For example, they roam around city streets where they have to rely on garbage from gutters for survival. A recent report indicates that large numbers of cows in major cities die due to eating plastic bags[30]. In some places, it is considered good luck to give a cow some snack, bread, or fruit before breakfast. A person can be sent to jail for killing or injuring a cow as per animal protection law. However, as most of India's cities have been overcrowded in recent decades, cow-friendly attitudes and policies have posed some problems. For example, Delhi city's 13 million people have to share the streets with 40,000 cows, often leading to complaints, since they spread trash by ripping garbage bags; they also dangerously obstruct traffic. Consequently, officials have employed cowboys to round up and the roaming cows to move them outside city limits, sometimes to special reserves where they are cared for. Although city leaders may not give up until the vast majority of the cows are moved out, sceptics argue that some of the cows return to their home turfs within days of being moved[31]. Cows are honoured across India at least once a year on the day of _Gopastami_ or the cow festival when they are washed

30   McNamee 2009
31   Chomchuen 2009

and decorated in the temple and given offerings with the hope that their gifts of life to humanity will continue. Nonetheless, animal activists complain that cows are being abused during transportation to slaughterhouses after long and torturous journeys in trains and trucks or on foot. Slaughtering cows is permitted in two states: West Bengal in the east and Kerala in the south. It is illegal to transport them across state lines. India's USD 2 billion leather export industry depends on 4,000 tanneries and leather-goods factories scattered across the nation; they depend on cattle. Therefore, the government overlooks the sacredness of the cow and continues to promote the leather trade. Animal activists suggest that lifting the ban on slaughter may deter the deadly illegal transport across state lines because poor villagers can no longer afford to keep unproductive cows and suppressing it may cause greater misery. However, such a drastic step may provoke the anger of the cow lovers of India, so politicians will avoid making any statements that might upset them.

The cow is the holiest animal in India and their slaughter is banned throughout India. The cow is one of the most worshipped animals in India, she is treated as the god in the shape of an animal. The cow is regarded even more than a mother in the sense that it fulfils all the needs of her children. The cow in India is believed as a gift of the gods to the people.

Monkey

In Hinduism the monkey deity, Hanuman, is a prominent figure in the Ramayana, a Hindu epic. A devout follower of Lord Ram who is an incarnate of Vishnu on earth, Hanuman is instrumental in bringing victory to Ram. Hanuman is associated with valour, strength and loyalty. He is a reincarnation of Shiva, the god of destruction. In orthodox villages, monkeys are safe from harm (Thomas 1911, p. 52). Monkeys are a revered species and are hence protected in India even today.

Chinese religions and mythologies give monkeys and ape cultural significance as metaphors for people. Chinese deities sometimes appear in the guise of monkeys, for example, *Sun Wukong* or "Monkey King" is the main protagonist in Wu Cheng'en picaresque novel Journey to the West. In *Daoism*, monkeys, particularly gibbons, were believed to have longevity like a xian ``transcendent; immortal'', and be innately adept at circulating and absorbing qi "breath; life force" through the Daoist discipline of *daoyin* "guiding and pulling". Similar to Daoism, Chinese Buddhism paradoxically treats monkeys as both wise and foolish animals. On the one hand, the Jataka tales say that Gautama Buddha was a benevolent monkey king in an earlier incarnation; and on the other hand, monkeys symbolized trickery and ignorance, represented by the Chan Buddhist "mind monkey" metaphor for the unsettled, restless nature of human mentality.

The Celestial Bird

Birds in the ancient civilizations of the world were symbols often raised to the ranks of deities. Probably the original god was Garuda-a great, golden-winged, mythical eagle from Tibet, the bird of life. destroyer of all, creator of all.

Garuda

Garuda, in Hindu mythology, is the bird (a kite or

an eagle) and the vahana (mount) of the god Vishnu. In Rigveda, the sun is compared to a bird in its flight across the sky, and an eagle carries the ambrosial soma plant from heaven to earth. According to Hindu and Buddhist stories, the  giant, birdlike Garuda spends eternity killing snakes like Nagas. The feud started when both Garuda's mother and the Nagas' mother married the same man. The husband then gave each one of his wives one wish. The Nagas' mother asked for a thousand children.

Garuda is described as golden yellow from his feet to his knees, white from his knees to his navel, scarlet from his navel to his neck and jet-black from his neck to his head. His eyes are yellow and his beak blue. His expression is fearsome and his hands are in the *abhaya mudra*. Another description states that he has eight hands, six of which hold a pot of ambrosia, a club, a conch shell and a discus. The *Visnu dharmottara* calls him *taksya* and it states that he should have a beak-like nose, forearms, face and round eyes, breasts, and legs of a vulture and two wings. The hands at the back hold a parasol and a jar of ambrosia and the hands in front are in the *anjali* pose. *Grunwedel* suggests that the parrot and the west-Asian griffin were the basis on which the modern iconography of the *Garuda* were developed but on earlier Buddhist monuments at *Sanchi*, *Garuda* is portrayed as a *mythical bird*. In the United States of America, the great seal also prominently features the eagle. A whole ancient religious treatise titled Garuda Purana and widely referred to by Hindus, elaborately deals with and codifies the rules for the deliverance of the dead. The practice of praying to Garuda is a living tradition in India. In Jagannath Temple, Puri, there is a pillar called the Garuda stambha, in front of the doorway to the sanctum sanctorum with a statue of Garuda atop the pillar. Devotees embrace the pillar believing in its acquired magical power because of the Lord's direct gaze on it. Birds, therefore, take on a whole new dimension in iconography and symbolism when one talks of the great mythical eagle Garuda.

Bees

The value of honey and honey bees was known to the inhabitants of the Indian subcontinent long before the dawn of the recorded history of this land. Evidence of beekeeping and harvesting honey in India can be traced back to the early Vedic Period (c. 1,500 BC) after the discovery of  a series of rock paintings in Bhimbetka, belonging to the Mesolithic or earlier period dating between 15000-11000 B.C.E. The paintings show crudely drawn semicircular combs sometimes surrounded or covered by bees[32]. It is clear that hunting for honey and its collection was one of the common activities among the Stone Age people of this period. In Āyurveda, a system of alternative medicine, honey is mentioned as being used for healing and cleaning wounds, anointing and diets. Ancient India's oldest sacred book, the Rig Veda contains several verses about the properties of honey as not just a sweetener but a medicine with immense potency to cure many diseases[33].

---

32 Dr. K.K.Kshirsagar; http://ancientindianwisdom.com/bees-and-honey-in-ancient-india
33 https://entomologymanchester.wordpress.com/2020/08/05/bees-and-their-symbolism-in-indian-mythology/

The bee, in her deified form, known as Bhramari, finds mention in Hindu mythology. The bee goddess Bhramari is an incarnation of Shakti and is the embodiment of strength and divine energies. The buzzing of the bee is likened to the humming of Vedic texts. It also is a symbol of romanticism and is supposed to act as Kāma's (the Hindu God of Love) subsidiary weapon in addition to his bow, the weapon of love.

In Catholicism, the Virgin Mary, often represented by Honey bee[34], is also known as the Queen of the Bees. In Ancient Egypt, it was believed that the tears of the Sun God Ra turned into bees upon touching the ground.

The animals that are listed are only a few most popular ones amongst a hoard of others. The list would be endless if all the animal totems of the indigenous natives of Africa, America, Australia and India are taken together. From a primitive hunter society to an agrarian then to an industrial and finally, to modern society, the development of man would not have been possible and cannot continue without his association with nature, complete with plants and animals. Yet, sadly enough, this association has also been the reason for the extinction of many animal species!

---

34 https://entomologymanchester.wordpress.com/2020/08/05/bees-and-their-symbolism-in-indian-mythology/

From the yore to contemporary, Nandi the Bull - an icon of worship, Brihadeshwara Temple, Thanjavur, India[35]

Statue of fox holding the symbolic jewel in Fushimi Inari, Kyoto, Japan. An anthropomorphic creature, the fox is believed to be the harbinger of wealth and good luck in Japanese culture.[36]

---

35 Photography Credits: Nataraj, R; Source- https://unsplash.com/photos/SzMR1Vcf5aw
36 Photography Credits: Karen Chew; Source - https://unsplash.com/photos/Fx0HP2S9gFQ

The Bull, known as Nandi, is considered sacred and is empowered with Divine attributes. Bull Temple in Basavanagudi, Bengaluru India[37]

Statue of Lord Shiva with Nandi, the Bull, in Chardham Temple, Namchi, Sikkim[38] Shiva, also known as Nageshwar, has snakes coiled around his neck.

---

37 Photography Credits - https://www.karnataka.com/bangalore/bull-temple/
38 Photography Credits - Spandan Pattanayak; Source:https://unsplash.com/photos/PpZobixj2KU

Wooden carving of a human, a snake and a bird on a cathedral door of The Malaga Cathedral in Spain[39]

The Statue of Goddess Sekhmet, one of the oldest known Egyptian deities, is depicted as a lion-headed woman.[40]

---

39   Photography Credits - Maria Lupan; Source: https://unsplash.com/photos/Z-Su4y_ao6o

40   Photography credits: Nacho Díaz Latorre; Source: https://unsplash.com/photos/nCNt1Mr9k-0

Image of Garuda in human form in the famous Golden mountain temple in Bangkok[41]

Garuda Pancasila, the national emblem of Indonesia [42]
Garuda, the vahan of Vishnu, is the celestial bird with immense strength

---

41 Photography credits: Agto Nugroho; Source: https://unsplash.com/photos/kfDsJyJJiZE
42 Photography Credits - Mufid Majnun; Source: https://unsplash.com/photos/iqm36Y14P5U

Garuda atop Aruna Stambha, Jagannath Temple, Puri, Odisha, India[43]

Horses on either side of the southern gate of Jagannath Temple Puri, Odisha, India[44]

---

43 https://en.m.wikipedia.org/wiki/Aruna_Stambha
44 http://www.shreekhetra.com/sripillar.html

Tigers standing guards on both sides of the entrance Western Gate/Tiger Gate/Vyaghra Dwara, Jagannath Temple, Puri, Odisha, India[45]

Image of the Bee Goddess worshipped in India[46]

---

45 http://www.shreekhetra.com/sripillar.html
46 Source: https://www.planetbee.org/planet-bee-blog//the-sacred-bee-bees-in-ancient-india-and-china-7tmcx#:~:text=Honey%2C%20Bees%2C%20and%20the%20Gods,life%2C%20resurrection%2C%20and%20nature

Kama, the God of Love, with his bowstring of bees[47]

The cow, considered the most sacred animal by the Hindus, is treated as a mother.

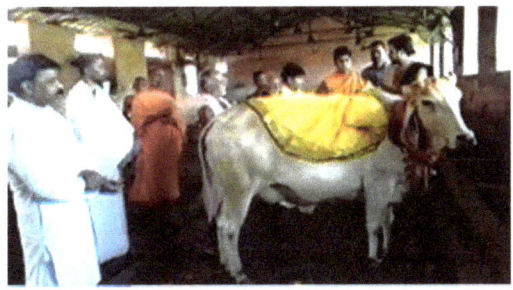

Cow Worship on Gopastami in Puri, Odisha, India [48]

---

47 Source: https://www.planetbee.org/planet-bee-blog//the-sacred-bee-bees-in-ancient-india-and-china-7tmcx#:~:text=Honey%2C%20Bees%2C%20and%20the%20Gods,life%2C%20resurrection%2C%20and%20nature

48 https://odishabytes.com/watch-gopashtami-festival-celebrated-in-odishas-puri-know-its-significance/amp/

Cow Worship in Nepal [49]

---

49   https://stillunfold.com/art-culture/10-animal-worships-from-different-cultures

CHAPTER FIVE

Hybrid Animal Icons: An Image of Mutual Respect and Coexistence

Nearly every culture has a mythology about a creature that is part man, part beast. In Western culture, such characters were first depicted in plays and stories from ancient Greece, Mesopotamia, and Egypt. They are possibly even older because sphinx, centaur, and minotaur mythology were likely passed down through the centuries by oral traditions especially kept alive through dance, music and theatre. In rural India, the tradition of folklore is kept alive by way of granny's bedtime stories in every household even today. In fact, the oldest  of the Vedic texts and Hindu mythologies are examples of oral transmission through millennia.

Though there are differing theories on the possible existence of such creatures, in reality, philosophers, historians and academia give, in substantial measures, the benefit of the doubt to the likelihood of such creatures being a figment of imagination. Primitive man would observe an animal that had a unique trait and the inexplicability would engender curiosity (Weissenborn, 1906b, p. 282).

The observation of this distinguishing characteristic caused the early man to be in awe. Because of this, early humans revered creatures with unique characteristics.(Weissenborn, 1906b). A wishful desire to possess such qualities as the flight of the bird, the power of the lion, the majesty of the horse, the calm patience of the elephant and many more animals caught hold of the fertile mind of humans and this created a fusion of creatures. Moreover, the notion that animals are divine manifestations, led naturally to the worship of hybrid creatures.

The mythical Greek horse-man known as the Centaur is one of the most well-known hybrid animals. One intriguing explanation for the creation of the centaur is that inhabitants of the Minoan society, who had no prior experience with horses, came across tribes of horse riders and were so amazed by their prowess that they invented tales of horse humans. Regardless of its origin, the centaur tale persisted into Roman times, when there was a vigorous scholarly dispute over whether the mythical creatures actually existed, similar to the debate over the yeti's or the chimaera's existence today. Since then, the centaur has continued to feature in literature, including the Harry Potter books and movies. There are the Pegasus and the Unicorn, two most popular horse

creatures from Greek mythology. Hippocampus is a huge fish-tailed horse which is supposed to be the progenitor of the sea horse of today. In Asian myths also horse hybrids hold a place of admiration. Horse occupied a prominent place in ancient Chinese mythology. Horse hybrids like the Llongma, a fusion of horse and dragon and Nuwa, a horse with a female human torso, are just a few. Hayagriva, an animal icon, with a horse head and a human torso, is a benevolent god in the Hindu pantheon. Temples are dedicated to him and Hayagriva is worshipped by people in some parts of India even today.

A hybrid of a bull and a man, the Minotaur appears in Greek and later Roman mythology. Its name comes from the bull-god Minos, who was a prominent figure in the Cretan Minoan civilisation, and from a ruler who required Athenian adolescent sacrifices to feed the bull. The Greek tale of Theseus, who battled the Minotaur in the centre of the labyrinth to save Ariadne, features the Minotaur's most well-known appearance. The mythical minotaur has endured, showing up in both contemporary fantasy literature and Dante's Inferno. A contemporary interpretation of the Minotaur, Hell Boy first appeared in comic books in 1993. It might be argued that the Beast character from the Beauty and the Beast story is a different manifestation of the same. According to some Puranas, the sacred Hindu texts, Nandi or Nandikeshvara has a bull-like visage and a human body. A statue of Nandi is placed at the entrance to the sanctum sanctorum of all Shiv temples. People pay obeisance to Nandi first before offering prayers to the main deity until the present.

The Sphinx is an animal with a human-like head, lion-like body and haunches, and occasionally eagle- and snake-like wings and a tail. As a result of the well-known

Sphinx monument that can be seen today in Giza, it is most frequently connected with ancient Egypt. But the sphinx also appeared in Greek mythology. The Sphinx is a perilous creature that can appear anywhere and asks people to answer questions, then eats them if they don't get the answers right.

The Sphinx plays a significant role in Oedipus' tragic story since he suffered greatly as a result of successfully solving the Sphinx's riddle. The Sphinx has a woman's head in Greek and Egyptian mythology, respectively. Similar to the sphinx is the Narasimha (discussed earlier,ch6)in Hindu mythology. He arrived to end evil and religious intolerance by vanquishing the demon monarchs Hiranyakashipu and Hiranyaksha. With lion-like features and claws, Narasimha is considered one of the Hindu god Vishnu's incarnations.

Every mythology includes mermaids, who are half human and half fish, but every society has its unique variation. The Cameroonian water spirit Jengu is a stunning figure who has a human upper body and a fish tail, long hair, and gapped teeth. Jengu is said to bring luck and healing to those who worship her. In Philippine tradition, the mermaids/mermen Sirena and Sireno watch over the water. The Sirena's seductive voice hypnotises fishermen and sailors, causing shipwrecks. Dagon is a Merman who is revered as a fertility god in Mesopotamia and Assyria. Cecelia is a female Sea Witch that lives in Lake Yaju, Japan, and is half octopus and half human. In India, Matsya, (discussed earlier,ch4) a half-human and half-fish, is revered and is believed to be the first incarnation of Vishnu, one of the most important gods in the Hindu pantheon. In literature, the Matsya finds mention in Jayadeva's, a Hindu poet of 12th-century composition, Gita Govinda. In contemporary literature, The sea lady by H.G. Wells, one of Wells's best novels though lesser-known works, is a fantasy novel featuring a mermaid.

For a practising Hindu, invoking Ganesha, the elephant-headed god, is a compulsive habit. Ganesha is the remover of obstacles, so he is worshipped before beginning any significant activity, including business, marriage, buying assets and childbirth. Many people interpret Ganesha's combination of an elephant head and human body as a metaphor for how the spirit ought to coexist with the natural world.

Nawarupa, also known as Byala (especially in Arakanese myths), is a hybrid mythical creature that is said to be a fusion of nine different animals. Its name literally translates as having "nine forms." The creature is described as having a prominent trunk like an elephant, horns like a rhino, eyes like a deer, ears like horses, wings like a parrot (or possibly its tongue), a body like a lion, a tail like a peacock (or yak), and feet like chinthe (the gryphon like creatures often depicted in Buddhist pagoda complexes). The current flag bearer of Myanmar uses the Pyinsarupa (literally, "five forms"), a legendary creature, as its heraldic emblem. References of a similar complex hybrid creature with nine body parts of different animals, called Nabagunjara[50] can also be found in the Mahabharata and other ancient literary texts of India.

Another similar interesting imaginary creation like the Chimaera, for example, with a lion's head, a goat's

---

50   discussed earlier, chapter 6

body, and a serpent's tail exhaling flames, can never exist in reality. Yet the word 'chimera' has been used to name biogenetically engineered fusion of plants by scientists. Botanists first used the term to describe grafted plants in the early 20th century, but it was later appropriated by other fields of study. In modern science, a chimaera is an organism that has different genetic components combined together. In other words, it has two sets of DNA, each of which has the instructions needed to create a unique organism.(Rachael Rettner 2016). Does it mean that there can be naturally born beings part human and part beast?

Whether it was for fear of beasts or fondness for animals, with bafflement one applauds the wisdom and imagination of the ancient people, who could represent their gods as a hybrid of humans and animals, leading us to believe in not only coexistence but the urgency for conservation today.

Buddha and the three headed elephant at Chachoengsao, Thailand[51]

---

51   Credit: Alice- https://unsplash.com/photos/JJD6m9X_ym0

The popular Ganesh - elephant in a human form[52]

A longstanding connection with apes, the theory of evolution. Hanuman the monkey god[53]

---

52   Credit: Unfold Memory
53   Credit: Sonika Agarwal- https://unsplash.com/photos/SP3HH-6MdNMc

Animal figures in the famous white temple of Thailand[54]

Dragon statue near Pashupatinath Temple Golden temple Kathmandu, Nepal[55]

---

54   Credit: Rach Teo- https://unsplash.com/photos/B7waLMPnh4s
55   Credit: Raimond Klavins- https://unsplash.com/photos/Wb5-rKL7ck4

Black dragon statue in Nansha Temple in Guangzhou, Guangdong Province, China[56]

Chinese guardian lion statue in front of Ancestral Temple of the Chen Family or Chen Clan Academy in Guangzhou, China[57]

---

56   Credit: Jean Beller- https://unsplash.com/photos/pkffh9_djUA
57   Credit: Joni Gutierrez- https://unsplash.com/photos/7S4FzjnxYHE

Human and Animal figures on top of Alte Bibliothek Old Library in Berlin[58]

Statue of a mermaid displayed on a rock by the waterside at the Langelinie promenade in Copenhagen, Denmark.Denmark[59]

---

58   Credit: Marie Bellando Mitjans- https://unsplash.com/photos/nXjQOWy22rM
59   Credit: Vita M- https://unsplash.com/photos/28_r3IxLDnc

*Angel of peace statue on the waterfront in Copenhagen, Denmark
A mythical hybrid creature of human with wings* [60]

Statue of Unicorns and a human figure standing in Canourgue Square, Montpellier, France[61]

---

60   Credit: Kasper Rasmussen- https://unsplash.com/photos/9cl0CpxyYnY
61   Credit: Nathan Cima- https://unsplash.com/photos/VZOFXb6wz3Y

Human and elephant guardians at Bhaktapur, near Kathmandu in Nepal [62]

CHAPTER SIX

The Indian Context

Indian literature and mythology are replete with stories and narratives of animals, birds, reptiles and even insects. In the Hindu, Buddhist, and Jain religious texts and scriptures 'Compassion to all' is the central theme that has been a guiding force in the lives of the people in the subcontinent. In these texts, animals are bestowed with divine powers. Gods can take different animal forms and in some cases, a fusion of animals or animal-bird or even man-animal-like creatures has found acceptance amongst people over millennia. Vishnu, one of the important gods in the Hindu pantheon takes the form of a fish, a turtle, a boar, a man-lion creature called the Narasimha and many more in the course of performing his godly duties. Shiva, another important god, happens to change himself into several forms of animals, birds, reptiles, insects male and female human forms. Kamadhenu or Surabhi, Hanuman, Nandi, Naga, and Sesha are names of animals such as the cow, bull, monkey, and snake assigned with

divine powers. That is Hinduism there is no distinct line of difference between gods, humans, the furred and the feathered, and the aquatic and invertebrates are reflected in hybrid gods like the Ganesha, Narasimha, Gandharvas, Makara, Uchchaihshravas, Sharabha, Navagunjara.

To endorse the fact about the importance of animals in our lives, we could look at this extremely fascinating mythological tale of the 'Nabagunjara', a 16th-century legend in Sarala Das' Mahabharata.

The Legend of 'Nabagunjara

[63] Agni the god of fire, consumed too much ghee(butter) So he was in excruciating pain. The excess ghee had to be used up by burning. But what is to be burnt? In order to end *Agni's* agony, Arjuna set fire to the luscious '*Khandava forest*', home to several species of animals and birds. As a result, a great many of them got burnt and an equal measure perished. In an attempt to salvage the rampage set by Arjuna Lord Vishnu incarnate, Krishna manifested himself into the *Nabagunjara*- a creature with the head of a hen crowned with *Brisaba's* hair, the neck of a peacock, waist of a lion, feet similar to an elephant, tiger, and horse, along with a snake's tail and hands of a man holding a lotus flower. This form of Krishna was a representation or was symbolic of the varying qualities possessed by different animals. The very appearance of Krishna in this form, dissuaded Arjuna in desecrating the forests further. The legend

---

63   Sarala Das' Mahabharata

of *Nabagunjara* is crucial in understanding the importance of animals in the Hindu tradition. Sarala Das' *Mahabharata* provides a brilliant imagery of the concept of Animals as icons. Lord Krishna's appearance before Arjuna as the mythical creature *Nabagunjara* that possessed nine differing qualities of nine different animals, symbolizes that one must be kind to animals, whilst learning and protecting them.

Interestingly, the *Nabagunjara* concept runs parallel to the concept of *Therianthropy* of French origin and is explained as "the mythological ability of human beings to metamorphose into other animals by means of shapeshifting".

Partnership of Man and Animal: Hindu Context

The interdependence of man and animal is too well- known and is certainly one of the core factors for the sustenance of life. All this gravitates to Gautam Buddha's foundational principle of *'oneness of life and environment'*

The Hindu religion generally considers all life forms as sacred . All species of creatures from the tiny insect to gigantic elephant are regarded as equally sacred (Agoramoorthy 2009a). The long list of sacred animals mentioned in the ancient Sanskrit scriptures cover major taxa, including invertebrates (bee, butterfly, mollusc, spider), fish, reptiles (crocodile, lizard, snake, squirrel, turtle), birds (eagle, falcon, crow, crane, goose, hawk, owl, peacock, swan, dove), and mammals (bat, bear, wild boar, buffalo, bull, cat, cow, dog, deer, elephant, fox, goat, horse, leopard, lion, monkey, rat, tiger, rabbit). Moreover, in Hinduism, the animals are sanctified by their association with the gods. Animals such as the swan, eagle and bull serve as the vehicles of the principal Hindu deities, namely Brahma, the creator, and Vishnu, the protector, and Shiva, the regenerator: all three make up the trinity of Hindu Gods. Some of the animals are sacred themselves, such as Hanuman, the monkey God, *Naga*, the snake God, and Ganesh, the elephant God. Major Hindu temples across India still maintain captive elephants since they play a role in religious rituals (*Majupuria* 2000).

Several mythical stories are associated with the sacred animals of India; for example, the eagle is worshipped while pigeons are the favourite animals of *Yamaraja*, the god of death. He rides on a bull water buffalo when he visits Earth. *Karthikeya*, the younger son of Shiva uses a peacock for his transportation while the goddess *Saraswati*, who possesses the powers of speech and wisdom rides a swan. Tiger is the vehicle of "*Maa Durga*". The crow is unique among birds as well since it is well-versed with the happenings in heaven, so people with desires towards paradise try to please it. The deer is associated with many mythical stories as well; Vayu, the air god's chariot is pulled by a pair of deer; Indra, the ruler of the heavens employs *Ucchaishrava*, a snow-white seven-headed flying horse as his vehicle. Similarly, the Sun god's chariot is being pulled by seven red horses (Waghorne 1999). Prehistoric animals such as the crocodile are also given importance in the religion. It is believed that the river Ganges depends on a crocodile for her frequent visits to the Bay of Bengal from the Himalayas. Moreover, the mythical elephant story is well-known: when an elephant named Gajendra was attacked by a crocodile while crossing a river, it screamed for God's help, and Vishnu appeared on his vehicle, *Garuda* (eagle) and destroyed the hungry reptile. Although there are 238 species of snakes throughout India, it is only the cobra with its two-eyed hood that is worshipped widely. The worship of snakes in India is intriguing. *Adisesha*, the king of snakes is the couch of Narayana, a form of Vishnu as he lies on the ocean. The snake can be seen around the neck of Shiva, the Hindu supreme God. Furthermore, snakes made of stone are found throughout most of the Hindu temples in India. In the western state of Maharashtra, a celebration called *Naag-Panchami* is specifically devoted to the worship of cobras. Similarly, snake worship is called *Jhampan* in the eastern state of West Bengal (*Gupta* 2006). The *Karni* Mata Temple is very popular as the temple of rats in Rajasthan.

Not only animals but rivers, trees, land and birds are also worshipped in Indian culture. Among the natural objects, the salagrama-stones (fossils of ammonite shells) are held in extraordinary veneration in India. People offer prayers to replicas of gods and goddesses made of stone that are installed in all temples. The Banyan, Peepal, Amla, Wood apple, and Banana trees are sacred. Every God has a weakness for specific flowers and fruits and so the trees bearing them are revered too.

A strikingly fascinating fact is that even today festivals and traditional rituals revering animals and plants are punctiliously practised in every nook and corner of India. Women circumambulating around a banyan or a Peepal tree for propitiation is a common practice. A lone tree, home to monkeys and birds, can be found inside the premises of many temples which are believed to be wish-bearing. Devotees throng to such places with a desire to get their wishes fulfilled with indomitable faith, defying logic and reasoning, even in the present times. The best part of such practices is that the offerings of bananas and coconuts to the trees provide food to the monkeys, birds and insects on the tree thus unconsciously continuing the practice of cohabitation.

The Cycle of Reincarnation: an Uncanny Resemblance to the Present-day

The concept of the reincarnation of Vishnu is interestingly intriguing since it represents in a way the theory of organic evolution involving animals. In order to indicate the aquatic origin of the life forms, Vishnu incarnates in the form of *Mathsya* (fish), followed by an amphibious *Kurma* (turtle). The next incarnation *Varaha* or wild boar is a terrestrial mammal, depicting how life transferred from the aquatic habitat to the terrestrial environment. Subsequently, *Narasimha* represents a beast's attempt to attain a human form, which is followed by *Vamana*, a pigmy human. In the incarnation of *Ramachandra*, perfect human qualities are identified, while the last one, *Kalki*, represents the human destruction of the planet giving poor attention to nature (Haigh 2006).

The Doctrine of Metempsychosis in Hinduism

A Hindu has no difficulty in believing that a beast, bird, or reptile may at any moment develop human features and functions. It is difficult for a believer in Hinduism to draw a line of demarcation between gods, men, and animals. Another interesting fact is that in many of the ancient Indian texts, all non-human characters including the animate and inanimate, are gifted with speaking abilities. There was communication between gods, humans and non-human characters, each in his language and yet understood by others. Jambavan, the bear, Hanuman, the monkey, Jatayu, and the eagle to name a few from the Ramayana, the characters of the Panchatantra, of the Mahabharata interact closely with human characters. These characters have helped the humans by winning a war, warning of imminent danger, nursing the injured and even sacrificing themselves to save their human friend or master.

If men depend upon animals, so also do the gods. Brahma is seated on a goose (*Hansa*); Vishnu on an eagle (*garuda*), which is a half-man; *Siva* on a bull (*Nandi*), Vishnu has at least ten *avatars* (incarnations) some of which are animals[64]. The study of iconography is conditioned by the study of religion, dance, temple architecture etc. Image worship forms the very pivot of popular religion in India. Image worship is practical and offers a good solution to the difficulty of conceiving a limitless Absolute. Animal worship may or may not be the most consummate kind of worship, but it is worship all-right, of the limitless being which is all-embracing.

In the modern world, animal worship has great relevance in the context of creatures big or small. The evolution process starting from an amoeba, the concept of ecological balance, preservation of nature and the rare species, respect for all living, transmigration of souls to other living creatures, meeting of *Aryan* culture with animistic and other cults that prevailed and still prevail among original inhabitants, are all part and parcel of the Hindu culture that to a large extent centre around animal icons.

Some Popular Animal Themes and Performing Arts

Set to *Jaydev's Astapadis* from his *Gita Gobinda*, an important part of the Odissi dance repertoire, the *Dasaavatar*, offers an enriched relish of animal depiction.

---

64 details on vahanas can be found in ch 7

The development of this dance form, says Reginald Massey, an eminent international scholar, is closely associated with that of religion. *Shaivite*, *Buddhist*, *Jain* and *Vaishnavite* temples in Odisha, some dating from as early as the 2nd century
BC., show sculptures and friezes of dance poses. Odissi dance draws upon these. This background may perhaps explain the heightened relevance of the worship of animal icons in Odissi through their depiction in the dasavatar item with its element of compassion and respect for all living creatures. Odissi also draws upon several ancient texts in Sanskrit and Odia. The most important among which are *Bharata Natya* Shastra, *Nandikeswara Abhinaya Darpana* and *Maheshwara Mahapatra Abhinaya Chandrika*. As for the accompanying music, the most popular choice is *Jayadev* Gita Gobind. The animal iconic depictions in Odissi (through *Dasavatar*) transcend the mundane and transport the *rasika* (the consummate viewer) to a world of magnificent aesthetic experience. The concept of *Dasavatara* by itself occupies a special place in the hearts of millions of Indians.

Ingrained into them from childhood these legends are the ones they grow up with. The legend of *Dasavatara* narrates the nine incarnations (*avataras*) of Lord Vishnu. The tenth avatar (kalki) which is yet to come represents the apocalypse or the end of this cycle of four yugas, the Satya, treta, dwapara and kali. Apart from other avataras like a dwarf, the huntersage, Lord Rama, Krishna, Buddha, and

Kalki we have animal icons. The fish, the tortoise, the boar, and the man-lion. In Odissi the presentation of *dasavatara* (ten incarnations) is often performed to *Jayadevs* celebrated composition *Pralaya payodhi jale..........jaya jagdisha hare* referring to the churning of the oceans.

Here one may mention that *Dasavatara* is linked to a large extent to yet another legend which is the churning of the oceans (*samudra manthana*). The story goes that as the tussle between *asuras* (demons) and *devas* (gods) continued and along with that the churning of the oceans the massive mountain began to sink to the bed of the ocean.

Both the devas and the asuras paled as they saw their efforts come to nought. Even as they watched they saw Lord Vishnu assume the form of a wonderful and gigantic tortoise. Plunging into the ocean he bore the mountain on his back, forming a mighty pivot. Seeing the mountain rise once more the faces of devas and asuras brightened and they resumed the churning. The huge mountain twisted and turned on the back of the divine tortoise. The lord later held down the mountains on the back of the tortoise and took up the serpent to churn the ocean.

Of the many incarnations of Vishnu next to the Tortoise comes the Boar. When the earth had slipped into the depths of the cosmic waters and was being submerged at the time of the final dissolution, Brahma sought the help of Lord Vishnu to rescue it. Lord Vishnu manifested himself as a tiny boar. Even while Brahma stood looking on, the boar grew in size. Seeing the gigantic boar, the sages and the devas realized that this was none other than Lord Vishnu, manifesting himself in the form of a boar to save the world. All these interesting details are exquisitely portrayed in Odissi dance.

Then comes the *Narasimha* (man-lion) avatar. *Prahalada*, a mythological figure said that when his father *Hiranyakasyapu* had left his mount *Mandhara* to practice austerities, Indra seized his mother suspecting her of carrying in her womb the child of *Hiranyakasyapu* the enemy of the Gods. Indra wanted to destroy the newborn child. But on the advice of *Narada*, Lord Vishnu dismissed the idea.

Prahlada exhorted all the asura boys to practice devotion to Lord Vishnu by treating every living creature as though it were one's own very self. This he extolled as the highest goal of man in the world.

Hiranyakasyapa was furious with his son *Prahlad* for being such an ardent devotee of Lord Vishnu. He leapt from his seat and took his sword and knocked at the pillar behind which Prahalad had taken shelter. The pillar split open and there appeared a man-lion. It was lord Vishnu who had assumed this form of half-man half-beast. This was *Narasimha*, who picked up *Hiranyakasyapa* and tore up his stomach dragging out his entrails, Vishnu then wore the entrails as a garland. All the residents of *kuntha* (heaven) thanked Lord Vishnu for saving them from the asura. All these are so magnificently portrayed by a skilled Odissi dancer, that the viewer is left absolutely awestruck.

The message here is important. The message is to enhance the *devalike* (Godly) aspect in us while overcoming and subduing the *asura* (devilish) tendencies and to also acknowledge the fact that animals like humans are both parts of the grand scheme of things.

We ordinary women and men in India respect and worship animals through many lived traditions. While the Odissi dancer depicts the eulogy through an enhanced aesthetic relish of lyrical and graceful movements, *Jayadev*, the grand composer immortalizes animal icons through his unparalleled compositions. Figuratively speaking, all of us sing paeans to animals in our own way.

The ten incarnations of Vishnu out of which four are in anthropomorphic forms
Painting of Jayadev Dashavatara[65]

---

65   https://en.m.wikipedia.org/wiki/Dashavatara

Carvings of animals associated with divinity and mythical human- animal celestial creatures in Mahabalipuram temple complex, Tamil Nadu, India[66]

Idol of Maa Durga and Tiger at Mumbai during the Navratri festival of 2019[67]

---

66 Credit: Mari Ganesh Kumar- https://unsplash.com/photos/3OWW1ya-CEY
67 Credit: Sonika Agarwal-

Statue of Nandi the bull in Pashupatinath Temple, Kathmandu, Nepal[68]

---

68 Credit: Raimond Klavins- https://unsplash.com/photos/dcXQuB-gNNT8

CHAPTER SEVEN

The Indian Context: Religion and Conservation

Religion is a powerful facilitator of the evolution of prosocial behaviour in human society. In many countries, religious beliefs have determined local resource use and facilitated the protection of species and ecosystems, governed to an extent by the voluntary involvement of local stakeholders. Although religious adherents are distributed unequally in relation to areas important for global biodiversity, in India there is an overlap between such areas and the religions of Buddhism, Hinduism and Islam. Circa 4 billion people in countries with biodiversity hotspots follow an organized religion, and these countries generally have low ecological footprints, with nearly 60% of people utilizing < 2 global hectares per person. In promoting environmental conservation this association provides an opportunity to work together that is more persuasive than the scientific importance of species. Sacred species and sites are also concentrated in biodiversity-rich nations; in India, for example, there are c.

50 groups of sacred animals, and more informal sacred sites than formally protected areas.

India is home to numerous religious groups, indigenous communities, ethnic groups and regional cultures, each with their own beliefs and taboos. Religions, especially those that have originated from the Indian subcontinent have long advocated  care and passion for nature and the environment, resulting in the protection of forest areas, aquatic bodies and various species. In Hinduism, many species are considered sacred because of their association with gods and goddesses. Lord Shiva (the destroyer), one of the three main deities of Hinduism, is represented with a spectacled cobra Naja around his neck, signifying that he has conquered death, and representing dormant energy (kundalini). Lord Krishna is one of the 10 incarnations of Lord Vishnu (the protector), another of the three main Hindu deities. In Hindu mythology, Lord Krishna is known for his fondness for butter, and one story tells how he hid stolen butter rolled within a leaf of the sacred fig Ficus religiosa. Basil Ocimum sanctum, known locally as tulsi, is also worshipped as a sacred plant, a favourite of Lord Vishnu; the annual ritual Tulsi Vivaha coincides with the start of the Indian marriage season.

Many faunal species are revered as vahanas, or vehicles that carry or transport gods and goddesses. The tiger is associated with the goddess Durga (the invincible), the peacock with Karthikeya (God of war), the owl and elephant with Lakshmi (goddess

of wealth, love, and prosperity), and crocodiles with the goddess Ganga (the sacred river). Similarly in Buddhism, meditating Buddhas (individuals who have attained enlightenment) and some bodhisattvas (those who practise the way of life of a Buddha) have an animal vehicle. The Bodhi tree Ficus religiosa under which the Buddha attained enlightenment is held sacred by Buddhists and is considered to be the tree of life.

Localized cultural attitudes and practices (e.g. sacred groves, the deification of bird, animal or tree species) attributed to indigenous and non-indigenous communities have facilitated effective biodiversity conservation. For example, the Bishnois, a religious sect in the state of Rajasthan, are ecologically conscious and do not cut trees or kill animals. Some Buddhist sects in the northeastern states and in the western Himalayan regions have evolved community conservation practices, including bans on hunting and fishing, like the black-necked crane Grus nigricollis, for example. The tribal communities of Kattunaickens, Kurumbas, Sholigas and Irulas living in the Nilgiri Biosphere Reserve who are primarily wild honey gatherers traditionally, treat the bees as sacred beings and hold prayers before going into the forest for harvesting the honey. And the most important fact to note is that they harvest only an adequate quantity, leaving enough for the bees to come back to the same place again. This is a perfect example of sustainability. Such practices[69] play an important role in the protection of threatened species. The belief in supernatural monitoring and punishment deters people from violating norms and breaking social rules and may have played a vital role in maintaining sacred sites in

69   https://india.mongabay.com/2020/03/could-tribal-honey-hunters-help-save-the-bees-and-improve-our-food-security/

India. It is also likely to have contributed to the conservation of freshwater fishes, which have been associated with supernatural beings.

Biogas, Manure and the Bovine

India harbours the largest domesticated bovine population (294 million) in the world which includes cows, bullocks, buffalo, and calves (Ravindranath et al. 2000; Tata Energy Research Institute 1997). Based on the mean annual average dung yield (fresh weight) of 4.5 kg/day for cattle and 10.2 kg/day for buffalo, the total dung production is estimated to be 659 tons annually, with cattle dung accounting for 344 tons and buffalo dung accounting Govindasamy Agoramoorthy, Minna J. Hsu: Only about 40% of the dung is used as fuel in rural areas. The quantity of dung used annually in the existing 2.7 million family-type biogas plants is estimated to be 22 tons.

Biogas technology can be an effective way of using cow dung to produce methane that can be adapted by rural people as fuel for cooking food items, with less impact on forest ecology. An added advantage is that the "slurry" or the residual matter can be used as a natural fertilizer for crops. The potential for household biogas units in India is 12 to 17 million. However, only 4 million biogas plants were installed by 2011. Thus, the impact of household biogas plants on sustainable development is yet to be fully realized in rural India (Ravindranath et al. 2000; Agoramoorthy & Hsu 2008). Firewood collected from forest areas still serves as the main fuel consumed in India and peoples' dependency on firewood has a serious detrimental effect on the local ecology due to the unsustainable removal of natural forest vegetation. Energy use projections indicate that India's rural communities will continue to use biofuel (firewood, dried dung, and biogas) while urban areas will switch to LPG, kerosene, and electricity (Sarma et al. 1998). We studied 125 household biogas plants in villages during 2001–2005 in three states, Gujarat, Rajasthan, and Madhya Pradesh in western India, to record data on the impact of household biogas plants on local ecology and community (Agoramoorthy and Hsu 2008). The biogas plants were established by a local non-profit agency, the Sadguru Foundation, to help rural people to promote natural resources management (Jagawat 2005; Agoramoorthy 2009b). Our study showed that the annual average reduction of firewood was 638 kg/household, reflecting a drastic reduction from 1048.9 kg before using the biogas plants to 410.6 kg afterwards. Each household's impact on the forest for firewood collection after the biogas plant was reduced to 61% (0.7 tons per household). A total of 80 tons of firewood from the natural forest nearby was spared by the 125 households each year. It clearly showed the enormous potential of household biogas plants in relieving ecological stress in forest areas of rural India. After people started using biogas, kerosene usage was reduced by 62% (from an average of 121 litres/year reduced to 46 litres/year. Interestingly, chemical fertilizer usage was also significantly reduced by 50% (from an average of 472 kg/year reduced to 235 kg/year) easing toxic pollutants on soil and the associated ecosystem (Agoramoorthy & Hsu 2008). Before the establishment of biogas plants in villages, the cost of firewood and kerosene in most households exceeded the annual salary of a rural Indian family. Thus, people were often forced to harvest firewood from the forest illegally. Biogas plants, being an eco-friendly affordable technology, safeguard local forest resources. The negative impacts of chemical fertilizers on soil and ecology are also well known (Hall & Robarge 2003). After the biogas plants were established in villages, the need for chemical fertilizers reduced, and farmers were seen increasingly using the organic slurry as a natural fertilizer for crops, which enhances topsoil health in agricultural areas promoting healthy agricultural and terrestrial ecosystems in villages. Organic manure helps in retaining soil fertility and productivity, especially in the ecologically fragile drylands of western India (Agoramoorthy 2009b).

Religion and Freshwater Fishes in India

Freshwater fishes have been considered sacred in many parts of India since the Vedic period. Species of mahseer (Tor spp.), for example, a threatened group of cyprinid fishes, are mentioned in various religious scriptures as being valued for propitiating the souls of deceased ancestors and relished by forest-dwelling saints. This reverence for mahseer continues and the fishes are protected in several stretches of rivers associated with temples, where fishing is prohibited and local communities, pilgrims and temple authorities help to monitor and safeguard the fish population.

Indian mythology and folklore always considered nature an essential part of human survival and gave animals, plants, and other non-human creatures equal, some and birds a sanctity that times even more important, as a man. Religious beliefs have endowed certain trees, and animals to endure in villages and tribal communities even today and save them from being destroyed. But now this happy, mutually beneficial relationship has begun to feel the strain of modern development.

India has the honour of being host to 1,200 species of birds out of a total number of 8,600 that live in the world. The great diversity of its physical features, climate  and vegetation gives a permanent residence to 900 species and lures 300 migratory birds to its fertile grounds during winter. She has a made-to-order range of forests and offers such a bewildering variety of landscapes that you can choose any kind you like. There are lofty snow-capped peaks in the high Himalayas with vast verdant coniferous forests nestling at their base. Beautiful unspool alpine glades where hundreds of rare wildflowers and plants grow are found in the remote high de valleys. The western region of the Himalayas has a cold, temperate climate with heavy snowfall and not much rain. Conifers like pine, deodar, spruce, and fir grow at different heights of the mountains. There are still huge, dark forests of old deodars and pines around hill stations like Simla, Chail and Nainital and some of the trees here are high as the hillside. Oaks, maples, and walnut trees are also seen here commonly, and the ground cover of the forest is a thick carpet of ferns and wildflowers like primulas, buttercups, daisies, wild poppies, lilies, and roses. The deep scarlet flowers of the Rhododendron add a splash of colour to the unbroken green landscape. But the eastern Himalayas have a much better display of these flowers since the forests here are denser and lusher. The moist, warm climate is ideally suited for orchids and femes and many other plants. Over four hundred species of orchids are found there growing on trees and also on the ground. The deciduous forests begin to take over as you step into the area beyond the foothills. The fertile soil of the Gangetic plains allows the trees to reach great heights and there are thick forests of Sal along with dense bamboo groves, along with trees like Shisham, Siris and  Red Silk Cotton. Mango and Jamun trees grow wild here and fruit abundantly to feed the birds and animals of the forests. The deciduous forests continue eastwards but if you travel west the scenery changes dramatically as the trees thin out. In the dry arid areas of Rajasthan, only the sturdy Acacia family can survive and many varieties grow here along with thorny shrubs and cacti. The babul, a common Acacia tree, is one of the most useful trees of the arid as 'kattha' which goes into the making of a pan. The Thar desert regions give fuelwood, fodder, resin, gum, and lac as well looms silently in the extreme west where there is nothing but unending stretches of sand dunes. The landscape changes back to green once more as one approaches the Deccan plateau. The dominant tree of these deciduous forests is Teak – and far away in Odisha, huge armies of the Olive Ridley turtles emerge from the sea and lay thousands of eggs on the beaches. The Indian Wolf howls in the remote lonely deserts and mountains and the Indian Pangolin curls up to ward off enemies but the Indian Python just swallows what comes its way. The list of fascinating animals of India is endless and each one of them is there in their safe habitat, waiting patiently for prey and maybe a few well-behaved admirers.

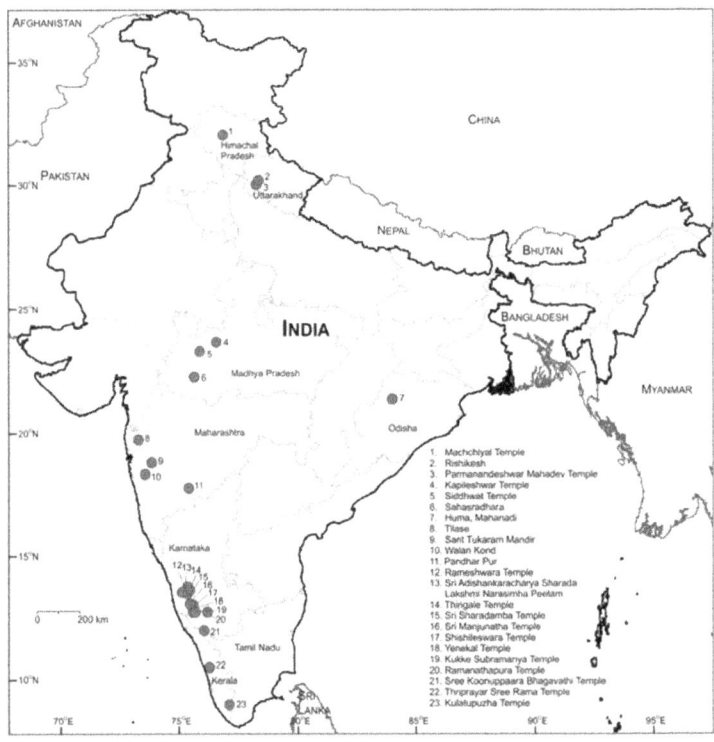

Fig. 1 Locations of important temple fish sanctuaries in India.

Plate 1 Temple fish sanctuaries in (a) Walan Kond (site 10 in Fig. 1), (b) Yenekal Temple (14), (c) Ramanathapura Temple (20) and (d) Shishileswara Temple (17). (a and b © Parineeta Dandekar; c and d © Shrinivas Kadabagere)

In Walan Kond (Savitri River) in the northern part of the Western Ghats, local people regard mahseer as the children of the goddess Parvathi (Katwate et al., 2014). On the Tunga River, also in the Western Ghats region, the Sringeri fish sanctuary protects threatened cyprinids of the genera Hypselobarbus, Neolissochilus and Tor. Chippalgudde Matsya Dhama, another sanctuary on the same river, protects, among other fishes, the endemic herbivorous cyprinid Hypselobarbus pulchellus, categorized as Critically Endangered on the IUCN Red List (Rema Devi & Ali, 2013). The fishes are considered sacred as they are associated with Lord Vishnu, whose first incarnation on Earth was in the form of a fish. In this incarnation, Lord Vishnu is believed to have saved the first human on Earth by informing him of the calamitous floods that were to follow. Many tributaries of the River Ganges are considered sacred, and religious sentiments play a positive role in the protection of the Endangered golden mahseer Tor putitora (Jha & Rayamajhi, 2010) in this region (Dandekar, 2011). Local worship of the fish god is a key driver of conservation at Machchiyal Lake in the state of Himachal Pradesh, where the fish are fed regularly by local people and tourists. The temple authorities keep the water free of pollution and prevent exploitation by local people (Plate 1).

The charismatic and threatened mahseer species are probably better protected in such sacred sites (Gadgil et al., 2001; Gupta et al., 2015) than in unprotected open-access areas, where they are subjected to indiscriminate (often destructive) fishing, and habitat loss as a result of hydroelectric projects and pollution (Pinder & Raghavan, 2013; Nautiyal, 2014; Gupta et al., 2014a). The mainstays of this protection are the prohibition of fishing in these waters, the availability of food (through artificial feeding), and active monitoring against pollution and other hydrological changes. Community-based educational programmes have improved the water quality in many temple pools by ensuring the protection of upstream and downstream reaches (Dandekar, 2011; Gupta, 2013).

Ecological and Socio-Political Issues

Although freshwater fishes are one of the most threatened vertebrate groups (Leidy & Moyle, 1997; Carrizo et al., 2013) they are often neglected in conservation efforts, including in countries rich in freshwater biodiversities, such as India. None of the 150 threatened freshwater fish species in India (IUCN, 2014) are legally protected or the focus of species-specific conservation plans. The increasing threat to freshwater ecosystems and fish species in India has been the subject of debate not only among scientists but also among stakeholders, including local communities (Gupta et al., 2014c). However, the role of stakeholders in freshwater biodiversity conservation is often overlooked by policymakers (Gupta et al., 2014b) as a result of an overt emphasis on centralization and adoption of a technocentric approach to managing ecological entities (Gupta et al., 2014b).

Despite the apparent conservation benefits of sacred sites, several ecological and policy-related concerns have yet to be addressed (Dudley et al., 2009). Providing legal status to sacred sites would help ensure additional protection for these areas but could also undermine the concept of religious values and traditions associated with the sites (Dudley et al., 2009) if local communities were allowed only limited access. The success of legally protected sites is often hindered by poor management and enforcement because of a lack of human resources (Kanagavel et al., 2013) and in some cases, the transfer of site ownership to Forest Departments has resulted in conflict with local communities, which has adversely affected site management

(Gadgil, 1991; Bhagwat & Rutte, 2006). To avoid this, the legislative arrangement should empower the primary stakeholders and uphold their rights and put land-use and management mechanisms in place rather than devolving and transferring management to the Forest Department. The legislation should promote the bio-cultural diversity of individual sites rather than focusing on biodiversity alone, given the interdependence of biodiversity and cultural values at these locations (Verschuuren, 2010). Sacred sites could also benefit from being integrated into a larger, state-level conservation landscape.

The most important environmental challenge related to temple fish sanctuaries is the need to manage their upstream reaches so that the sacred sites are not damaged by stressors that originate in other places. One way to achieve this is through the establishment of safe zones where sustainable and regulated fishing activity is promoted, potentially yielding social and economic benefits for local stakeholders (Gupta et al., 2014b). Another emerging question is whether temple sanctuaries serve as arks (where fish can mature, reproduce and help repopulate adjoining areas) or cages (where they can survive but are unable to reproduce because of unsuitable habitat or other hindrances; Kumar & Devi, 2013). Whether temple sanctuaries alter the life history traits (e.g., feeding behaviour, reproduction) of fish is, therefore, a priority for future research. There is also a need to explore non-invasive means of monitoring and stock assessment, such as the use of hydro-acoustics or video cameras.

Many community-conserved fish sanctuaries at Indian temples are threatened by the proliferation of hydropower projects (e.g. Nakur Gaya and Hosmata in Karnataka, and Walan Kond and Tilase in Maharashtra; Dandekar &

Thakkar, 2015). Environmental impact assessments do not even mention the existence of such fish sanctuaries, nor are the communities managing the sanctuaries involved in making or implementing decisions related to dams (Dandekar & Thakkar, 2015).

The erosion of religious beliefs, an increase in religious heterogeneity, and changing traditions are potential drivers of the increasing threats to sacred sites (Gadgil, 1991; Bhagwat & Rutte, 2006). In promoting freshwater conservation through temple fish sanctuaries linkages between religion, culture and conservation (McKay, 2014) must be highlighted in a non-discriminatory manner to avoid causing divisions among people of different religions, which could have an adverse effect on conservation efforts.

The bio-cultural conservation of freshwater fishes should not be limited to temple sanctuaries but expanded to include individuals, communities or organizations interested in facilitating and coordinating such initiatives. However, informal institutions such as temple sanctuaries serve as models for the survival and dissemination of beliefs that support the conservation of nature, habitats, and species. These beliefs could be retold as simple stories that emphasize their positive value, and not the religion from which the beliefs originate. However, to achieve long-term conservation benefits it will be necessary to inspire people to put their beliefs into action.

Research suggests that sacred spaces harbour species of scientific importance in significant abundance, and in many cases these are the last remaining relics of the original landscape and species (Dudley et al., 2010). Although not all temple sanctuaries necessarily harbour endemic and threatened freshwater fishes, it is the pro-conservation beliefs in place that are of significance and should be harnessed to promote freshwater fauna and habitats, regardless of the species involved. Conservation organizations could focus attention primarily on those sacred spaces that encompass critical habitats and species, and establish partnerships with faith groups to assist in the fulfilment of conservation goals (McKay, 2014).

The Way Forward

Temple sanctuaries continue to exist in India but diminishing dependence on traditional dogmas may mean that religious beliefs and taboos are unlikely to be prioritized in the future (Bhagwat & Rutte, 2006). This is particularly pertinent in the case of marginalized communities living along riverbanks, for whom fish is a cheap source of protein, and fisheries a livelihood option. Incentive-driven conservation (Hutton & Leader-Williams, 2003) in the form of national recognition and provision of financial support for maintaining or improving the water quality at sanctuaries could ensure that such informal protected areas provide much-needed protection for threatened freshwater taxa. There is a need for a greater understanding of the short and long-term socio-economic, environmental and conservation impacts of such sacred sites (Berks, 2004). With the current dearth of conservation options for freshwater biodiversity (Strayer & Dudgeon, 2010), whether sacred sites can be supported legislatively and utilized as an additional safeguarding mechanism can be ascertained only through rigorous scientific studies that involve locally relevant stakeholders.

Novel Initiatives

C Srinivasan is the Project Director at Indian Green Services. He is an expert in Zero Waste Management across

India and his famous Solid and Liquid Resource Model (often called the "SLRM Model" or "Vellore Model") has been widely acclaimed as the national model for Zero Waste Management after his success with a hill restoration project at Vellore. He has been involved with many projects in this field and is currently working with a number of states in India toward effective waste management.

Many such initiatives are coming up. It's time that India comes of age in protecting its fauna and its entire environment.

In India, animal worship and the rituals that go with it present a consolidated scenario where compassion and care reign supreme. The most interesting fact is that all this is part of a lived tradition that sends definite messages of love and compassion for different kinds of animals.

What has to be noted here is that humans are far from doing a favour to animal kind. In fact, what is true is that the very survival of humans depends on the preservation of flora and fauna and the environment in general. The sooner we realize the gravity of the matter the better it would be for us humans. We may probably have to devise novel methods to achieve our objective. One of the methods could be through employing soft power, besides other options that are already available. The defining feature of soft power is that it helps to get across to people easily and is a great cannon in our arsenal.

The world's religions have made a contribution to environmental conservation and sustainable development.

Many organisations and individuals are associated with world religion and have in the process promoted sustainable development and environmental protection. One of the notable examples is Oxfam (Oxford Committee for Famine Relief) which was initiated long back in 1942.

Another example is WWF (World Wide Fund for Nature), which in 1986 initiated a dialogue with five of the world's most prominent religions—Buddhism, Christianity, Hinduism, Islam, and Judaism—about how the tenets of their faiths could help environmental conservation. The World Bank has since been working with faith-based groups to reduce poverty and promote conservation in the developing world. A growing body of literature has suggested that conservation and development are both driven by ethical or moral values and can earn legitimacy through cultural acceptance, public engagement, and mass support.

The WWF-India has created a countrywide awareness of environmental problems and has actively campaigned to set up a number of wildlife sanctuaries. It has been supporting many eco-development projects and has a series of specific programmes in areas like Species Survival, Pollution and Energy Conservation, Urban Ecosystems and Environmental Legislation. But though India is trying hard to save the environment, hundreds of problems continue to exist as the population of the country rises alarmingly and resources get increasingly limited.

Men and nature are now at loggerheads, each trying to survive at the cost of another though belated efforts are now being made to involve the rural  people when planning conservation programs. Though now there are stringent laws to deal with environmental pollution and the Government has passed an Environment Protection Act which awards higher penalties and even shuts down industries causing pollution, the lack of trained manpower to enforce these laws has made them toothless and ineffective. But there are successful conservation stories too which bring a ray of hope for the future.

Project Tiger, launched in 1973, brought fresh ideas to conservation in India and saved not only the tiger but huge areas of its wild habitat. As a result, a number of other animals and plant species got a new lease on life too. As its home was protected and allowed to regenerate, the tiger flourished and from a dwindling population of 2,000, it sprang back to 4,000 in 1988. The government now plans to start Project Elephant to restore the Earth-shaking geological events that took place around 70 million years ago, created the varied landscapes of the Indian subcontinent and gifted it with an incredible and rich variety of natural wealth.

The existing Wildlife Protection Act is to be made even more strict to stop the illegal trade in animals and to control poaching. Handicapped by limited funds and innumerable other pressing problems, India is still trying to save its environment and restore the balance between man and nature that existed not so long ago.

So the saga of the worship of animal icons has historicity and points to the immense potential of putting in place a well-knit world order that is the crying need of the day.

CHAPTER EIGHT

Animals as Vahanas (mount or vehicle) of Deities

Vahanas – The Rides of Hindu Gods and Goddesses

The Hindu gods and goddesses have a specific animal or bird species on which they travel. One can relate these animals or birds, known as *Vahanas,* to the vehicles we use today. But then, unlike modern vehicles, these *Vahanas* were adept at moving through air, space, land and sea. These vehicles of God, whether animals or birds, represent the different spiritual and psychological forces that identify each deity. The gods used *Vahanas* mostly for war and travel.

No Brahmanical deity of the Puranic pantheon is known either in the dhyana or in artistic representation to exist without his or her proper mount. Like the *ayudhas*[70] the mount or the vahana, as it is called in the iconographic texts, is a cognisance typical of or peculiar to the deity concerned. Images of Siva are almost invariably associated with his mount the bull; those of Kartikeya always go upon the peacock, and the images of Vishnu, but for seldom exceptions, show his mount Garuda upon the pedestal. Mounts are found as unavoidable adjuncts of the

---

70 Ayudha generally translates to weapons; but, in shilpa-sastra, the term indicates whatever objects the idol holds in his or her hands.

iconographic representations of the medieval and post-medieval age.

Vahanas of the gods and goddesses

Most of the *Vahanas* of gods and goddesses are worshipped by Hindus with offerings and prayers. The relationship between a god and a mount is not that of a master and a servant, but more like that of a father-son or body and soul relationship.

A walk through a few gods and their Vahanas

Brahma – Swan

God *Brahma* has a chariot *Hamsa* (Swan). It represents intelligence, insight, judgment, skill and creativity. The word "*Hamsa*" is a combination  of two words, "*aham*" + "*sa*". It means "I am he". The *hamsa* bird is beautiful, peaceful and graceful. This indicates that Brahma is the creator and master of all beauty and grace in the world. The *Vedas* also mention that the bird can separate milk from water. This means that *Brahma* can help us transform our intelligence and knowledge to distinguish between good and evil.

Saraswati – Hamsa (Swan)

Goddess Saraswati is the consort of *Brahma*. Her *Vahana* is also the *Hamsa* .. *Saraswati,* the goddess of knowledge and education rides the *Hamsa*, a mild and exquisite hen that  stands for its beauty, elegance, poise, and dancing skills.

Indra – Airavata **(A White Elephant)**

The typhoon god "Lord *Indra*" incorporates thunderbolts as his guns and is considered the harbinger of rain to the earth. *Indra* is a critical god of *Aryan* warriors. His Vahana Airavata is a splendid white elephant regularly depicted with 4 tusks.

Shiva – Nandi **(The Bull)**

Lord *Shiva* is one of the outstanding deities of Hinduism. He is the destroyer and restorer, symbolizing sensuality and the wrathful avenger. His mount Nandi stands for sexual energy – *kama* and fertility. Riding on its back, Shiva has the energy to govern all impulses.

Durga – **Lion or Tiger**

Goddess *Durga* is the unconquerable shape of *Devi*. She is the ideally suited god and is additionally recognized as *Parvati*, the mother of Lord *Kartikeya* and Lord *Ganesha*. *Durga* is visualised as a warrior girl with more than one arm wearing guns, *mudras*, or symbolic hand gestures, driving a lion or tiger.

Vishnu – Garuda **and** *Adi Shesha*

Vishnu, "The Preserver," is one of the predominant deities of Hinduism, who's seated on *Adi Shesha* and additionally rides on the Eagle King, *Garuda*. According to Hindu Scriptures, *Adi Shesha* or *Shesha Naga* holds all planets and earth on his hoods. As in line with the

Mahabharatha, Adi Shesha was born to sage *Kashyap* and his spouse, *Kadru*. *Garuda*, a deity himself, is regularly shown as winged with a human form and a beak-like nose. *Vishnu* mount incorporates *Vishnu* to *Vaikuntha* (Heaven), wherein he lives. His mount *Garuda* stands for wisdom and swift speed. Hence, if one desires to have these qualities, one must worship Lord *Vishnu*.

Lakshmi – Uluka (Owl)

Maha Lakshmi is the goddess of success, fortune, prosperity, and wealth. Interestingly, her *Vahana* the Owl is known as *Uluka*. Her *Vahan – Uluka* presents an image of persistence and intelligence.

Ganesha – Mouse (*Mooshak*)

It is believed that a demon by the name of *Mooshikasura* was wreaking havoc in the world and the gods had sent

Lord *Ganesha* to fight him. Even before Lord *Ganesha* attacked the demon, he went down on his knees and prayed to the Lord for forgiveness. Lord *Ganesha* decided to forgive him under one condition he has to serve him forever. The demon accepted the condition and Lord *Ganesha* turned him into a mouse. This is how *Mooshikasura* the demon became *Mooshak* the *vahaan*.

Kartikeya – Peacock

Lord *Kartikeya* is also known as *Murugan, Subramaniam, Sanmukha*, or *Skanda*. He is the second son

of Lord *Shiva* and Goddess *Parvati*. He is also known as the **god of war**. *Kartikeya* is a popular deity in the southern part of India. He is embodied in perfection, a brave leader of God's forces, who was born to destroy the demons. He has the *Vahan* Peacock.

Agni (Fire) – Ram (Goat)

The god of fire, *Agni*, is one of the main deities of Hinduism. God *Agni* is always seen riding the Ram. *Agni* is shown riding the *Ram* and rarely, a chariot pulled by goats. Some versions also talk about *Agni* riding a chariot pulled by horses. The *Ram* signifies power, strength, and vitality. The vibrancy of *Agni* is also reflected in the vehicle he chose for himself, the *Ram*.

Surya Dev – Seven Horses

In Hindu *dharma*, the *Surya Deva* gives light to the world. He is the father of *Kasyapa*, and her wife is *Chhaya Devi*. The god sun represents willpower, health, fame, and vitality. The sun is also known as *Ravi, Pusha, Aditya,* or *Grahapati*.

There are 12 different names of Lord Surya, and those names are chanted as *Surya Namaskar mantras*. The god sun rides seven horses, representing the seven *chakras* or spiritual centres in our subtle body.

Yama – Buffalo

In Hindu Dharma, Yama is known as the God of Death. One with red eyes, a club, and a noose in his hands, he rides the Buffalo as his Vahana. In Visnu Puran, Yama is depicted as the son of the sun god Surya and Sandhya (Daughter of Vishwakarma).

Maa Ganga – Makara (Crocodile)

Goddess Ganga is worshipped across the country. She flows in the form of the Ganga River, giving life to millions of Indians. She is considered the mother of all and the most sacred river. She can remove all sins of the person who takes a dip in her holy waters. The Vahana of goddess Ganga is a Makara, a Crocodile.

Shani – Vulture, Crow, and Raven

Lord Shani refers to the planet Saturn and is one of the nine heavenly objects as Navagraha in Hindu Astrology. He is one of the most worshipped  deities in the Puranas and looks like a black figure carrying a sword in his right hand and sitting on either a Vulture, a Crow, or a Raven. He is considered the god of bad luck and is also popularly called Ara, Kona, and Kroda.

Hanuman – (He Does Not Have a Vahana)

Lord Hanuman is one of the most worshipped gods by Hindus. Hanuman helped Lord Rama defeat the Asura- King Ravana of Lanka. It is believed that Lord Hanuman did not need a Vahana because he could fly himself and go anywhere.

Mounts or *vahanas* are not confined to the gods of the Brahmanical pantheon, and as such the concept of divinities being endowed with *vahanas* is not restricted to the Brahmanical order. Both the Buddhists of the Mahayana sect and the *Jainas* conceived their deities as having different *vahanas* of cognizance in each case. The conception, it may not be unreasonable to think, had been inherited from a common source and a common idea. A student of iconography would like to find out the distinctive mount of each particular deity, but no treatise on iconography explains the phenomenon clearly. Consequently, no recent authority on the subject has made any serious effort in clarifying the purpose served by these *vahanas*.

Hindu Goddess Lakshmi, flanked by elephants, on the wall of Kali temple in Puri, Odisha India [71]

---

71 https://www.dreamstime.com/royalty-free-stock-photos-goddess-lakshmi-image-hindu-wall-kali-temple-puri-image40454338

Monkeys are a common sight in the temple complex of Galtaji Mandir[72]

CHAPTER NINE

Important Temples of Animal Worship in India

If Remy, a lovely rat chef from Pixar's *Ratatouille*, lived in the Indian state of Rajasthan, there is a place where he'd be welcomed with open arms and reverence. The place is **Karni Mata** Temple in the small town of *Deshnoke*. The rat competition would be tight for Remy though, more than 25,000 rodents call this temple home. The rats not only live there but also consume food alongside humans. It's all because of *Karni Mata*, the deity of the local *Charan* caste whose male sons were believed to be reincarnated as rats. All her followers treat rats as sacred creatures, and this temple is a place to show their respect.

For an unprepared person, the temple may be intimidating. Should you plan to visit, know that you'll be surrounded by thousands of rats, and you'll be required to remove your shoes.

There is a temple in the Southern Indian state of Kerala that stands on a tranquil lake surrounded by palm trees and tucked away from civilization. The only lake temple in the state, it's a charming structure, though an unremarkable one in a country known for striking religious architecture, save for one thing. There is a real crocodile living in the pond. The reptile's

name is **Babiya**, and it is believed to be around 70 years old, and no one actually knows how it ended up in the temple's lake. Local priests say *Babiya* is a vegetarian and feed it a bowl of rice twice a day. So far this lake beast hasn't complained about the menu as there has never been a  single crocodile attack here. Sometimes *Babiya* is allowed inside the temple to participate in a service to the cheers and amazement of the visiting crowd. Florida's alligators should definitely take notice.

Hidden in the crevice of Aravalli Hills just a 10-minute taxi ride from Jaipur, **Galtaji** Temple is a sight to behold. A sacred place for Hindus, it is a mesmerizing complex of ancient shrines and seven holy pools cascading in the middle of the rocky terrain. But visitors come here not only for the spectacular architecture but also to meet the monkeys that live on the premises of *Galtaji*. Hundreds of macaques and langurs accompany people that come here for a prayer or a sacred dip. Be careful though, the primates may look cute and playful, but cross the line and you can get bitten or find your personal belongings snatched.

It's one thing to have sacred animals inside the temple, it's another thing to have a temple entirely in the form of a sacred animal. Of course, India has the latter covered, too. Deep in the country's heartland, in the state of Telangana, you can find the **Naga Devatha** Temple, which is designed to look like a giant orange snake with a flute-playing Hindu god Krishna on top of it. But it doesn't stop there, it's  time to enter the building. Once inside, you find yourself in a snake's belly following a tube-like tunnel full of various characters from the story of the Hindu gods Krishna and Narasimha. The snake behind the temple's design is *Kaliya*, a serpent from *Mahabharata* (an ancient Indian epic) that was terrorizing the Yamuna River dwellers before Krishna appeased it.

Tucked away from the business centres and modern glass-clad high-rises of Bangalore lies the ancient Bull Temple or **Dodda Basavana Gudi**. The cow is a sacred animal in India and worshippers can visit a temple with a 15-foot-tall idol of a giant bull (known locally as *Nandi*). The animal was carved from granite more than 500 years ago and still stands strong today.

In the middle of the lush state of Chhattisgarh, this temple devoted to one of the most powerful Hindu goddesses, **Chandi**, may at first glance appear to be just another beautiful spot. But wait until the afternoon when the bears show up. Yes, really, the wild sloth bears come here daily to participate in the prayer services and amaze the crowds of temple visitors. The plot twist is that the bears aren't restricted by anything except a few men who look to ensure that the creatures don't cause any trouble. As unusual as it may sound to some, such a close coexistence of bears and humans has become normal for parts of India as more wildlife terrain is encroached upon to make way for urban development.

Formerly known as Madras, Chennai is a must-visit destination to get introduced to the culture of South India. Deep into its labyrinthine streets, you'll find the spectacular **Kapaleeshwarar** Temple, a complex of intricate towers, mysterious shrines, an artificial reservoir, and a kaleidoscope of figurines of all kinds depicting characters from the Hindu sacred texts. Known as one of the best examples of the ancient Dravidian architecture typical for South India and Sri Lanka, *Kapaleeshwarar* also boasts a great number of animal idols, including numerous cow statues on the entrance towers, a bull shrine, blue elephant figures inside the temple, and colourful peacocks wherever you look.

You may be a dog lover, but you will probably never get to the level of love that the people from the remote *Agrahara Valagerehalli* village south of *Channapatna* in Karnataka state have for the canines. Dogs here have a temple and are venerated by the locals. Although quite small and extremely hard to find, this shrine may well be one of the few places in the world where dogs are actually worshipped.

The building is relatively new, probably built in 2010 (even the villagers themselves are said to be puzzled about the origins of the **Dog Temple**) by a local businessman alongside a bigger temple to Kempamma, a village goddess. Inside you'll find two cute brown and white dog statues who regularly take part in colourful religious services. It is believed that the dogs bring good luck and protect the locals from all evil.

A jewel in the crown of the UNESCO-protected Khajuraho Western Group of Monuments Temple Complex, **Varaha** Temple is one of the most impressive animal temples in the country. First of all, it was built more than 1,000 years ago, around the year 900. Secondly, inside you find an imposing five-foot-tall idol of a wild boar with countless small statues of Hindu gods and goddesses carved on its sides.

It is a shrine of *Varaha*, the animal avatar of the god Vishnu in the form of a boar. According to a legend, Vishnu shapeshifted into *Varaha* to prevent the vicious demon *Hiranyaksha* from destroying Earth. *Varaha* succeeded and now we can marvel at the intricate beauty of this animal shrine his followers erected to celebrate the victory.

Those who choose to explore the picturesque *Mandaragiri* Hills on a day trip from Bangalore will be pleasantly surprised to find a fantastic **peacock-tail-shaped** Jain temple in their footsteps. Beautifully placed to complement the surrounding nature, the building is 265 feet of a colourful, Instagram-friendly spectacle. The peacock is a sacred bird for both Jainism and Hinduism, so you can find various depictions of it all around the country. The temple near *Tumakuru* may well be the most generous tribute to this bird. Apart from the Peacock Temple, be sure to hike up the Mandaragiri Hills for another Jain shrine and enjoy the scene-stealing views of the tranquil countryside.

[73]The temple of Goddess **Uttershwari**, located in a narrow bylane of Paikasahi village, Jagatsinghpur, appears like any other temple in the area. The 'bhog' offered to the deity, however, is what sets it apart from other temples in the State. Here, the Goddess accepts liquor and fish to cure her devotees of diseases like epilepsy.

Located in Ibirisingh panchayat of Tirtol tehsil, Odisha, the temple was built by the then zamindar Kanungo Krupasindhu Das. A Brahmin Janardan Pani, who used to

---

73   Amarnath Parida, The New Indian Express, 2018

eke out a living by begging, once dreamt of a goddess telling him that she would stay in the village and cure people of many diseases. Pani told Das about his dream and he constructed a temple in the name of Goddess Utterswari. The temple was damaged in a cyclone that took place in 1967 and a new one was built with Pani as the priest.

One day, Pani suffered from seizures and fell unconscious in the temple. He was cured after taking the 'bhog' of the Goddess. He then started offering fishes and Somarasa (alcohol) to appease the Goddess. Later on, people started offering liquor and fish to the deity to cure their children suffering from epilepsy. Today, devotees in large numbers bring their children to the Goddess to cure them of epilepsy.

The puja paraphernalia they offer contains flowers, fruits, and a small bottle of alcohol. One can get a variety of liquor near the temple, be it wine or whiskey. The priest opens the liquor bottle and puts half of the content in a shallow plate which is placed near the mouth of Goddess Uttershwari. Chief Priest of the temple, Banambar Mishra, said after fish and liquor are offered to the deity, the 'prasad' is distributed to people and children suffering from epilepsy.

"Then, the affected people and children are caned amid chanting of mantras to cure them of epilepsy and other diseases," he added. Sarpanch of Ibirisingh, B Bandana Das, said earlier devotees used to offer liquor during the daytime but now, this has been restricted to nighttime to check anti-social elements near the temple. Considering the uniqueness of the temple, locals have been demanding the construction of the main gate, a boundary wall and lighting arrangements around the temple. No help from any quarter has been forthcoming though.

A rare **Bee Goddess** Durga temple can be seen in Kateel near Mangalore, in the state of Karnataka. Situated on a green islet in the middle of the river Nandini, the presiding deity is Sri Durga Parameshwari. It is said that during the early part of Kaliyuga a rakshasa named Arunasura  was stung to death by a big, furious bee that is 'Bramara[74]' who was the Goddess in the form of a bee. Jabali Maharshi invoked the goddess by performing abhisheka with delicate coconut water and implored Bramaraambika to favour the world in her Saumya Roopa (delicate stance). At that point, the Goddess showed up in her Saumya Roopa amidst the stream where the present temple is built.

Karnimata Temple[75]

---

74   https://en.m.wikipedia.org/wiki/Bhramari
75   https://www.fodors.com/world/asia/india/experiences/news/photos/10-astounding-indian-temples-where-animals-are-adored

A temple for rats, Karni Mata Temple[76]

Garuda Statue, Atharnala, Puri[77]

---

76   DAVID EVISON/SHUTTERSTOCK
77   https://commons.m.wikimedia.org/wiki/File:Garuda_Statue,_Puri._Odisha.jpg

Sculpture of Garuda in front of Puri railway station[78]

Where live fish is offered to the deity, Uttershwari Temple, Jagatsinghpur Odisha[79]

---

78   https://www.123rf.com/photo_28101346_february-8-2014-puri-orissa-india-sculpture-of-garuda-in-front-of-puri-railway-station.html

79   https://www.orissapost.com/shrine-where-brandy-is-offered-as-prasad/amp/

CHAPTER TEN

Preservation of Nature: Promotion of Biodiversity - a Life-Affirming Fact

An Act of Reparation called for

All hope is not lost. As they say, *Better late than never*. Man has woken up to the reality of the irreparable damage caused to the environment by his actions. Though late, the realisation is slowly seeping in; it is time for us to react. The beginnings of small acts of redemption, initiated by organisations and individuals have started working on animal protection. If the remnants are to be retained, they have to be protected and conserved.

By 1972 and the first United Nations Conference on the Human Environment, public awareness of environmental degradation led to the development of the second generation of environmental agreements and institutions. Policymakers began to realize that many of the world's common pool resources could only be protected through international cooperation. Over the next 20 years, dozens of agreements were developed, with specialized international environmental organizations to implement them. A second major United Nations environmental conference in Rio de

Janeiro in 1992 marked a shift in natural resource policy, as the issues of environmental sustainability and economic development overshadowed concerns about pollution. But most observers believe the consensus of the Rio summit has not been fulfilled. Although a general agreement has been reached on the issues of global climate change, biodiversity, and the protection of marine resources, little progress has been made in slowing the pace of environmental deterioration. There is particular concern that international governmental organizations have been unsuccessful in adopting major conventions to conserve natural resources, which are being rapidly depleted as developing nations of the South seek the same living standards and consumer goods as the industrialized nations of the North. More importantly, major conventions have been adopted and ratified but no IGOs have been created or assigned the task of implementing them. Most observers believe natural resource protection is characterized by a sizable gap between rhetoric and reality. Sustainable development is now the dominant framework for international agreements at virtually every level. The difficulty of achieving economic growth—a goal of both industrialized and developing nations alike—without having an adverse effect on the environment, is becoming more and more apparent. The North/South split between developed and developing nations is likely to continue—a dynamic that will affect upcoming negotiations on natural resource protection. Developed countries, like the US, have recommended that developing nations do more to reduce consumption, while the US itself continues its own consumption patterns. Poor nations expect that the richer countries of the world, which are responsible for much of the current deterioration of the earth's resources, should pay for the damage from the past. In the meantime, richer developed nations look at that damage and seek to reduce any further loss of resources by expecting the poorer countries to learn from their mistakes. Over the years, several reforms of the existing structure of global environmental governance have been suggested, emphasizing the need to increase the UNEP's limited staff, resources, and support. The proposals have often been coupled with calls for additional reforms in the environmental mission and activities of the World Bank and the International Monetary Fund. In 1989, prior to the Earth Summit, New Zealand made an innovative proposal to the United Nations General Assembly calling for the creation of a global environmental organization, the Environmental Protection Council. Unlike existing UN bodies, the proposed organization would have a legislative structure empowered to make binding decisions on global environmental issues. New Zealand's ambassador called upon General Assembly members to adopt the proposal, arguing that "nothing less than an institution with this status will command the necessary respect and authority to achieve what is required." The proposal was seen as preferable to granting additional powers to the UNEP or creating separate agencies to deal with specific environmental issues. However, it is clear that there remains a lack of a clear mechanism for effecting change in the approach of individual states to the protection of natural resources. While the philosophical and political debate over sustainability continues, the major international governmental organizations are failing in their efforts to stop the further degradation of the planet. On this count sensitisation of youth in particular and people, in general, is an urgent need. As a step to induct children in their formative years the school curriculum may be restructured to include awareness of saving the planet. As the saying goes 'Catch them Young'.

EPILOGUE

Back to Roots

The idea of this initiative through academic activism is not to revoke or revive animal worship but to restore the foundering reverence to the fauna around us. It is not to soft pedal zoolatry but to emphasize the core value behind animal worship and its relevance today. The need of the hour is to admire the intelligence of the savage man and to be humble enough to take ancient wisdom seriously in understanding the necessity of cohabitation with all creatures big and small, meek and ferocious, wild and tame. Somewhere in our long journey towards civilization we forgot to stay gratified for the bounty of nature, the exigency of the universe, and the beauty surrounding us; we lost the ethos of our existence. As they say, we can learn our lessons well only in the face of punishment. The pandemic, global warming, pollution hazards, landslides, floods, extinction of some species of flora and fauna, isolation and detachment of friends and family are a variety of warning signals asking for a change in man's attitude and approach in his relationship with the environment. We are poised on the path of negating ourselves. Let that not take roots.

What is done cannot be undone. The only form of reparation is to preserve what is left with us. We need to act now with promptness and a clear objectivity clear objectivity, instead of taking a meandering path to reach our goal. We need to take the first step and time will teach how to take the strides. We need to resurrect the lost practices, sans violence, of Veneration of the Fauna and Flora. Veneration of the Fauna and Flora in no sense is a fad. It is a call of the day to open our eyes wide to life-affirming facts. The clarion call is loud and clear. It is now or never. To be or not to be.

The concern for the planet is certainly growing among the cognoscenti, yet a lot more needs to be done. It is heartening to note that the National parks of USA are recently being promoted in a big way by Barrack Obama the well-known humanist. John Muir the American nation's most forceful voice for preservation has impacted efforts that are to be reckoned with. When wonders of the natural world link up to culture, traditions and societies in a big way, that is when things turn to make a dent on the grievous issue of saving the planet with fauna or flora at its core. This is a foundational question concerning the planet as a whole and additionally what should be borne in mind along with this is the beautiful Hindu concept – *Vasudhaiva Kutumbakam* (the world is one big family).

Coming to the home terrain, apart from the gigantic initiatives taken by the Govt. of India and some commendable efforts by a few NGOs, we have the leading organization WWF that takes care of Animal conservation. The remarkable work they do should come to the limelight. More importantly, the school children should be exposed to such information. This would go a long way in sensitizing the children regarding this burning issue and can yield gratifying outcomes. One can sum up with the following lines, *"Come forth into the light of things, let nature be your teacher."* **-William Wordsworth**

References
1. https://www.planetbee.org/planet-bee-blog//the-sacred-bee-bees-in-ancient-india-and-china-7tmcx
2. https://en.m.wikipedia.org/wiki/Chinese_zodiac
3. https://en.m.wikipedia.org/wiki/Shaligram
4. https://www.animallaw.info/article/attitude-towards-and-application-animals-traditional-chinese-culture-0
5. https://en.m.wikipedia.org/wiki/Chinese_folk_religion
6. https://www.ncbi.nlm.nih.gov/pmc/articles/PMC6952866/
7. https://www.firstthings.com/article/2012/04/man-the-religious-animal
8. https://www.animallaw.info/article/attitude-towards-and-application-animals-traditional-chinese-culture-0
9. https://entomologymanchester.wordpress.com/2020/08/05/bees-and-their-symbolism-in-indian-mythology/
10. https://www.legendsofamerica.com/na-totems/
11. https://www.legendsofamerica.com/na-facts/
12. https://www.halalwatchworld.org/animal-welfare-in-islam
13. https://muslimhands.org.uk/latest/2021/07/animal-rights-in-islam-mentioned-in-quran-and-hadith
14. https://en.m.wikipedia.org/wiki/Animals_in_Islam#:~:text=According%20to%20Islam%2C%20animals%20are,prevent%20it%20from%20harming%20people.
15. https://www.peta.org/blog/how-muslims-can-help-animals-in-the-new-year/
16. https://www.esdaw.eu/animals-in-islam.html

17. https://courses.lumenlearning.com/suny-fmcc-boundless-worldhistory/chapter/pre-islamic-arabia/#:~:text=The%20Bedouin%20tribes%20in%20pre,%2Fwool%2C%20and%20other%20sustenance.
18. https://www.britannica.com/topic/Native-American-religion
19. https://www.discovermagazine.com/planet-earth/please-stop-using-the-term-spirit-animal
20. https://www.amacad.org/publication/indigenous-americans-spirituality-and-ecos
21. https://www.google.com/amp/s/theculturetrip.com/south-america/peru/articles/the-spiritual-importance-of-the-condor-puma-and-snake-in-peruvian-history/%3famp=1
22. https://authenticgathazoroastrianism.org/2011/07/11/157/
23. https://brill.com/view/journals/soan/18/4/article-p367_3.xml?language=en
24. https://www.speakingtree.in/allslides/10-worshipped-animals-from-around-the-world/246442
25. https://www.scientificamerican.com/article/3-human-chimeras-that-already-exist/
26. https://www.britannica.com/topic/Matsya-Hinduism

Peacock is the national bird of India [80]
The gorgeous beauty of the peacock has enamoured man throughout the ages. Photo credit: Ricardo Frantz

Nabagunjara in Patachitra painting by Shri kalu Charan Barik. [81]
Photo credit: Abhimanyu Barik.

---

80 https://unsplash.com/photos/GvyyGV2uWns?utm_source=unsplash&utm_medium=referral&utm_content=creditShareLink

81 Source: https://fundamatics.net/ecological-consciousness-and-the-tale-of-the-nabagunjara-from-folk-odisha

About the Author

Dr. Monica Das, retired Associate Professor of Economics at Gargi College, Delhi University, was a Fellow at the Developing Countries Research Centre, Delhi. She was a visiting scholar at UBC (University of British Columbia, Canada) in 2000. She has been a member of the USA-based International Association for Feminist Economics (IAFFE) for twenty years and currently serves on its select committee. She has presented research papers and chaired sessions at international conferences in the USA, Canada, Australia, and the UK under IAFFE's auspices. Dr. Das has numerous works to her credit including those published by Penguin and Harper Collins. Her book 'Selected works of Fakir Mohan Senapati,' published by Central Sahitya Akademi, received acclaim. She is the Chairperson/Managing Trustee of Fakir Mohan Foundation and directed the award-winning telefilm 'Anvesan' sponsored by Prasar Bharati. Dr. Das has served on committees and as a jury member for Doordarshan, India's television channel. Her deep concern for the environment and biodiversity led her to publish the book 'Animal Icons,' and her articles on Indian art, heritage, and the environment have appeared in prestigious publications. She has travelled extensively, including a recent trip to Mexico to explore Mayan relics.

Black Eagle Books

www.blackeaglebooks.org
info@blackeaglebooks.org

Black Eagle Books, an independent publisher, was founded as a nonprofit organization in April, 2019. It is our mission to connect and engage the Indian diaspora and the world at large with the best of works of world literature published on a collaborative platform, with special emphasis on foregrounding Contemporary Classics and New Writing.

www.ingramcontent.com/pod-product-compliance
Lightning Source LLC
Chambersburg PA
CBHW061209070526
44583CB00025B/3169